AF239762

KULTURWISSENSCHAFTLICHE ZEITSCHRIFT

Herausgegeben von der
Kulturwissenschaftlichen Gesellschaft

Heft 2/2022

FELIX MEINER VERLAG
HAMBURG

Bibliographische Information der Deutschen Nationalbibliothek
Die Deutsche Nationalbibliothek verzeichnet diese Publikation in der
Deutschen Nationalbibliographie; detaillierte bibliographische
Daten sind im Internet über ‹https://portal.dnb.de› abrufbar.

ISBN 978-3-7873-4333-1 · ISBN eBook 978-3-7873-4334-8
ISSN (Print) 2751-3106 · ISSN (eJournal) 2451-1765

© Felix Meiner Verlag Hamburg 2023
Druck: Books on Demand, Norderstedt
Printed in Germany

Inhalt

Editorial

A b dieser Ausgabe, dem Heft 02/2022, erscheint die *Kulturwissenschaftliche Zeitschrift* nicht mehr länger, wie seit ihrer Gründung 2016, bei De Gruyter Poland/ Sciendo, sondern nunmehr im Verlag Felix Meiner. Für die Entscheidung zum Verlagswechsel gab es produktionstechnische wie auch publikationspolitische Gründe. Im Abwägungsprozess der Frage, ob es sinnvoll sein könnte, die *KWZ* bei einem neuen Verlag zu publizieren, ist uns sukzessive klar geworden, dass der technische und der politische Aspekt eines wachsenden Unbehagens miteinander zusammenhängen. Zum einen hatte sich bei uns wiederholt der Eindruck eingestellt, dass die letzten Jahre von einer Tendenz zur Entleerung der Beziehung zwischen Verlag und Zeitschrift geprägt waren, insofern jenseits der finanziellen Abwicklung von Verlagsseite kein Interesse daran festzustellen war, die *KWZ* gemeinsam zu einem qualitativ hochwertigen Medium der deutschsprachigen und internationalen Kulturwissenschaften zu entwickeln. Ein Bemühen darum, in irgendeiner Weise auf die Inhalte der *KWZ* einzugehen, war nicht vorhanden. Das zu konstatierende maximale Nichtverhältnis zu einem etwaigen Ethos geistes-, kultur- oder sozialwissenschaftlichen Publizierens führte in Verbindung mit einem digital standardisierten Produktionsprozess und einer unübersichtlichen Auslagerung der einzelnen Produktionsschritte dazu, dass die Redaktion viel Arbeit in die Qualitätssicherung investieren musste. Dies mag man – zumindest aus der Perspektive der beteiligten Redaktionsmitglieder – beklagenswert und vielleicht sogar ärgerlich, weil unnötig finden, weit schwerer wiegt aber der zweite Grund unserer Entscheidung: Angesichts der aus unserer Wahrnehmung problematischen Effekte, die das gegenwärtige »Publikationsregime«[1] hinsichtlich von Themenselektionen, Publikationsfrequenzen und Forschungspraktiken auf die akademische Forschung hat,[2] ist unser Schritt zum kleineren Traditionsverlag Felix Meiner durchaus auch der Versuch der Artikulation einer Kritik am Geschäftsmodell der Großverlage im Sinne Michel Foucaults, nämlich »nicht auf diese Weise und um diesen Preis regiert zu werden.«[3] Dass die *KWZ* damit nicht komplett aus dem auf die Gewinnung und Verwertung von Daten ausgerichteten Publikationssystem und der es ermöglichenden

---

1 Vgl. das entsprechende Heft »Publikationsregime« der Zeitschrift *Mittelweg* 36, H. 2 (2022).
2 Mit Blick auf die Geistes-, Kultur- und Sozialwissenschaften vgl. Spoerhase, Carlos: Filetierte Vernunft. Veröffentlichungen in den Geistes- und Sozialwissenschaften. In: *Mittelweg* 36, H. 2 (2022), S. 4-13.
3 Foucault, Michel (1992): *Was ist Kritik?* Berlin: Merve, S. 12.

digitalen Ökonomie aussteigt, ist offensichtlich. Wohl aber glauben wir, dass der Schritt weg von einem der drei den deutschsprachigen Markt dominierenden Verlage – Springer, De Gruyter, Brill – und hinein in eine andere, an der wissenschaftlichen Praxis interessierten und ihr zugewandten Verlagskultur zumindest einen kleinen Unterschied macht. Open Access in der Hand weniger, auf Profitmaximierung ausgerichteter Großverlage ist eben kein Open Access, kein freier Zugang mehr, wenn sowohl Autor*innen und Herausgeber*innen wie auch Leser*innen durch Veröffentlichungs- und Zugangskosten potentiell von der Wissenschaft ausgeschlossen werden. Konzeptionell und von ihrem wissenspolitischen Anspruch her bleibt die *KZW*, was sie bislang auch schon war: eine über ein Peer-Review-Verfahren qualitätsgesicherte Zeitschrift, die aufgrund des Engagements der DFG und der *Kulturwissenschaftlichen Gesellschaft* über ein Open-Access-Modell eine Möglichkeit eröffnet, als Autor*in wie als Leser*in themenoffen und unbehindert von finanziellen Zugangsbeschränkungen an der aktuellen kulturwissenschaftlichen Debatte zu partizipieren und diese mitzugestalten.

Birgitt Röttger-Rössler, Boris Nieswand, Monique Scheer, and Thomas Stodulka

Cultural Diversity!?

A Roundtable

ABSTRACT: In the context of a roundtable held at the international conference ›Diversity Affects – Troubling Institutions‹ organized by the CRC Affective Societies in May 2021 at Freie Universität Berlin four social and cultural scientists critically discussed the meaningfulness of the term ›cultural diversity‹ and debated about the question whether the term ›culture‹ has transfigured into a leftover-category that lumps together the conceptually uncanny, politically uncomfortable, and empirically enigmatic. This article is the edited and revised transcript of this thought-provoking conversation.

KEYWORDS: cultural diversity, notions of culture, superdiversity, multicultural bodies, moral affects, culturalism

In contemporary social and cultural anthropologies one can identify a tendency towards an adjectival usage of the term ›culture‹. This term, which is not only a central concept in anthropology, but also in social and cultural sciences in general, increasingly appears only in collocations like ›cultural plurality/multiplicity/variety‹, ›cultural diversity‹, ›cultural heterogeneity‹, or ›multiplicity of cultural orientations‹, ›diversity of social and cultural backgrounds‹, ›plurality of cultural norms and practices‹, or the like.

The well-attended roundtable on ›Cultural Diversity!?‹ provided an interdisciplinary platform to reflect on the origins of adjectivising culture and discuss what these adjectival collocations might actually denote. Held at the Biennial Conference of the Collaborative Research Center 1171 »Affective Societies«, titled ›Diversity Affects – Troubling Institutions‹ on May 29, 2021, the Center's spokesperson Birgitt Röttger-Rössler asked three colleagues with disciplinary backgrounds in migration sociology, historical anthropology, and social and cultural anthropology, whether the term ›culture‹ has transfigured into a leftover-category that lumps together the conceptually uncanny, politically uncomfortable, and empirically enigmatic. Monique Scheer, Boris Nieswand, Thomas Stodulka, and Birgitt Röttger-Rössler critically debated the analytical value of the terms ›culture‹ and ›diversity‹.

Birgitt Röttger-Rössler: It is a great pleasure to welcome you all to this roundtable session. We will address an old but nevertheless pressing question, namely, what is culture and what do we mean precisely when we talk about cultural diversity? Furthermore, we will talk about the affective dimension of living cultural diversity and of researching it. I am glad to have highly distinguished guests for this roundtable discussion, whom I want to introduce now very quickly. First, a warm welcome to Monique Scheer, who is professor of historical and cultural anthropology at the University of Tübingen, where she currently also serves as vice rector for international affairs and diversity. Among her research interests are religion, secularity, and cultural diversity in contemporary Germany, the history of emotions and cultural theory. A warm welcome also to Boris Nieswand, who is a professor at the Department of Sociology, likewise at the University of Tübingen. His research focuses on migration, diversity, morality and cities. In one of his recent research projects, which is part of the CRC »Threatened Order« at the University of Tübingen, he investigates social relationships in ethnically and socially heterogeneous contexts, more specifically in highly diverse urban districts in Santiago de Chile and Johannesburg. His methodological approach may be characterised as reflexive and ethnographic. Last but not least, a very warm welcome to my dear colleague Thomas Stodulka, who is junior professor for psychological anthropology at Freie Universität Berlin and co-founder of a European Network for Psychological Anthropology. His work focuses on affect, emotion, childhood and youth, social inequality, marginality and mental health, datafication, as well as methods. He is specialised on Indonesia, where he conducted long-term field work; he also acted as co-director of the interdisciplinary project ›Researchers' Affects‹, which investigated the impact of affects and emotion on the research process.

More than 20 years ago, the social anthropologist Adam Kuper stated that social anthropologists normally get highly nervous when it comes to discussing the concept of culture. With this remark he pointed to the fact that any contestations about the definition of culture provoked deep irritations and feelings of uncertainty among scholars of social and cultural anthropology, but also of related disciplines. In my opinion, this anthropological nervousness not only still exists, but has increased considerably during the last 20 years. Anthropologists still have a highly ambivalent relation to the core concept of the discipline. In contemporary writings one can identify a tendency to use the term ›culture‹ primarily as an adjective in word compositions such as ›cultural plurality‹, ›cultural variety‹, ›cultural diversity‹, ›cultural heterogeneity‹ or ›diversity of social and cultural backgrounds‹, and so on and so forth. On the one hand, this linguistic practice of, as I call it, ›culture denominalisation‹ can be read as an expression of insecurity, which originates from the justified criticism of an essentialising understanding of culture as a territorially bound, homogenous and rather stable entity. On the other hand, it is associated with the growing usage of the term ›diversity‹ which has occurred as a distinct category to describe processes of inner social differentiation and plurality in the context of migration. Studies of diversity argue that it is necessary to look at a variety of criteria in order to grasp the increasing diversity of the so-called ›superdiversity‹, a term coined by Steven Vertovec, of contemporary societies.

One of the concept's variables besides age, gender, legal status, path of migration, education, ethnicity, language, religion, is subsumed as ›cultural norms and orientations‹. But what exactly do these categories mean? What do categories like cultural norms and orientations comprise? What do they denote precisely? In other words, culture as an adjective becomes transfigured into a kind of leftover category that lumps together the conceptually uncanny. So in my opinion, it is time to reflect once again about our usage of the term ›culture‹ in social anthropology as well as in sociology and cultural studies. Accordingly, we will, in the first discussion round, talk about the meaning and analytical value of the term ›culture‹ and then, in a second round, turn to the affective dimension of cultural diversity and discuss questions like what does it mean emotionally to live or work in culturally diverse settings?

Let us start with Boris Nieswand. Boris, you stated in one of your writings that it is impossible within the field of migration studies to discuss culture without getting enmeshed in discourses about discrimination and exclusion. So what does culture refer to from the perspective of a sociologist who works particularly on migration, and why is the term so contested in migration studies?

Boris Nieswand: Thank you very much, Birgitt, for inviting me and also for giving me the opportunity to say something on culture. I would first like to answer your question as a sociologist. Following Andreas Reckwitz (2015), it can be said that the concept of culture first of all opens up a contingency perspective on social life. It enables us to see that everything – even what appears to us as mere fact or self-evidently true – must be viewed as result of processes of meaning-making and understanding. Regardless of how we understand or represent something, it can always be understood and represented differently, by another person, in another place, at another time. Evidently, this concerns also us as researchers. To become reflexive means in regard to our own practice to incorporate the knowledge of the contingency of our own knowledge into the process of knowledge production. Somehow ironically, it seems that within the process of becoming more reflexive, the concept of culture becomes the means of its own abolition. Reflecting on the consequences of the contingency perspective leads us to realise that the concept of culture itself is contingent. If we use it in the Reckwitzian way, we don't use it in the Herderian way, we don't use it in the Bourdieusian way. Recognising that the employment of the term ›culture‹ is not sufficient to specify what it means or what it instructs us to do, we are prompted to look for more concrete aspects of social life or social fields that can be seen as expressions or indicators of culture: meanings of words and gestures, habitualised and embodied practices, the materiality of social life, cosmological views, discourses, gender or kin relations, myths and other iconic stories, rituals, arts and museums, patterns of interaction and so forth. However, specifying culture might at the end make us realise that we don't need the word ›culture‹ itself to address these more specific issues. Especially, if we are recognising that these other concepts seem to be less contested and mobilise less resistance. If we understand culture as a ›facilitator‹ of a perspective of contingency, it is perhaps a Wittgensteinian ›ladder‹, a tool that we don't need anymore when it has increased reflexivity about the contingency of knowledge and its consequences for our own professional practice. But why does the use of culture appear to be more controversial than other concepts? I would like to answer this question from my position as a migration scholar. The problematic relationship of migration studies is related to its potential to be used as a political means of ›othering‹, excluding and devaluing migrants and their descendants. Verena Stolcke (1995) wrote already in the early 1990s that culture has replaced the concept of race within the political right as a key concept. The reference to the right of collective cultural self-determination is used to protect nativist privilege and assign migrants an inferior symbolic and material position within the nation-state. Looking at the Identitarian movement, the AFD or PEGIDA and their anti-Muslim discourse, it becomes evident that Stolcke's analysis is still valid: culture is still a key concept of political right-wing extremism and right-wing populism. One might object that scholars should defend their concepts against political appropriation, that the phenomena which an anthropological concept of culture addresses will not disappear if we don't use the word anymore and that culture, properly used, challenges rather than reproduces racism and xenophobia. I think these arguments are valid, but would object that, once such a suspicion is in the world, it takes constant effort and justification to defend one's analytical language. And then the question is: do I want to deal with this suspicion or are there conceptual alternatives that work for me? You quoted Adam Kuper at the beginning, who argued that it might be better to use more specific terms than culture. I would add, it also helps to avoid intellectually unproductive debates whether the term itself is problematic or only some of its political instrumentalisations. And perhaps the 21st century no longer needs a concept of culture like the 19th and 20th centuries.

Birgitt Röttger-Rössler: OK, thank you very much, Boris. Let me try to wrap up your argument: you say that the notion of culture might be useful to reflect on the contingency of all knowledge, but that we do not need the term anymore. We can go on with using culture just as an adjective or not even this. You are proposing that instead of talking of a group's culture we should better speak of the group's particular knowledge, values, lifestyles, beliefs and behaviour conventions. In the second part of your answer it became clear that your unease with the term has a lot to do with its current misuse by certain political actors like the Identitarian movement and others. But is the essentialist use of the concept of culture by certain ideologically guided actors sufficient to abandon the concept even within social and cultural sciences?

Thomas, may I pass this ball to you? Do you agree with Boris? What does culture mean from the perspective of a social and cultural anthropologist whose research focuses on social inequality and marginality?

Thomas Stodulka: Thank you. Well, first of all, thank you very much for the invitation, it is great talking about culture, and thank you for this wonderful introduction. I will try to contradict you, Boris, although I am aware of all the difficulties of the culture concept. First, defining culture as relational is crucial, meaning that the very term itself is related to the audiences that we speak to. When talking about culture in an interdisciplinary collaboration with psychology, for example, I self-identify as a scepticist that resists cultural essentialism. Although these audiences and arenas are different, I am still the same person, so I would like to give an integrated answer first. There are lots of reasons for culture theorists and anthropologists, particularly from a postcolonial theory perspective, to dump the concept due to its stereotypical essentialisation and its potentialities for the discrimination of ways of life, persons and communities based on their phenomenological appearance as assumed ethnicities, gender, sexual orientation or age, to name just a few that, once charged with nationalist public rhetoric. They are played out rhetorically as ›culturally different‹ in a negative way and instead of understanding diversification as enrichment to thriving societies, we realise as scholars that culture seems more frequently operationalised negatively, pointing to a deficient lack instead of an empowering abundance of something. So, the concept of culture is inherently paradoxical, as it seems both loved and hated in different social sciences and cultural studies.

Interestingly, it was precisely in the 1990s, when anthropology lost interest in further discussions of culture as a concept, that it re-emerged in related disciplines such as cultural psychology and cultural studies. Social and cultural anthropologists have preferred to avoid the term for decades, particularly since the prevailing entity of culture and ethno-locality have been deconstructed in the face of globalisation and mobility phenomena and theories. The discipline's shift from villages, communities, and neighborhoods as primary units of analysis towards activities, imaginations, connectivities and multi-localities has countered essentialism and ethnocentrism, but it has left the culture concept theoretically orphaned; even worse, we have surrendered and left the culture concept to right-wing intellectuals so that it could grow into this ›xenophobic monster‹. When using the term ›culture‹, and I can already anticipate resistance in the audience today. If we debate culture as a concept at all, we do so on affective battlefields laden with moralised arguments on why culture is ›anachronistic‹ and such a ›bad‹ and ›outdated‹ concept, or perspective to look at contemporary worlds; why and how it is essentialising heterogeneous and diverse human experience, behavior and speech, promoting ethnocentrism that at best leads to a social and political hierarchisation of persons and communities, but actually only redefines historicised stereotypes based on colonial, racial and ethnic descriptions that lead to discrimination, stigmatisation and marginalisation. I feel this theorisation redefines the arguments of ultra-conservative and rightwing movements, who promote the same meta-narrative and operationalise it for racist and discriminating political agendas. Many colleagues have argued that there are only cultural particularities, or that the culture concept cannot be used any longer to account for the subjectivities, historicity and intersectionality of contemporary conviviality. I am inclined to advocate the opposite. Like power, as Foucault has illustrated, I want to argue that culture might best be understood from its resistance, not only in epistemic terms, as to why politically engaged scholars reject the culture concept altogether with its theoretical potentialities. More importantly, contesting the centralised public and political abstractions of ethno-localised and racialised culture conceptions, the concept of culture itself is a powerful political and epistemic tool to ask very precise and concrete questions. So, what notion of culture is it exactly that is juxtaposed at the intersection of belonging and not belonging? Which phenomena are activated by nationalists and which are neglected and hidden from public debate? What is the culture that is used by not only right-wing parties in their attempts to establish hegemonic narratives based on blood and soil rhetoric? I feel that it is precisely due to this contested quality of culture that I am inclined to argue that the concept of culture can provide a significant anthropological arena of political engagement. It should not be left to radical nationalists to drive their wooden horses filled with xenophobia and racism into Troja. Through the contestation of cultural lenses, we can see fundamental societal arenas of power struggles over citizenship, appropriation, exclusion, exploitation, and violence to name just a few. We need discursive spaces of culture and cultural diversity so we can not only identify political currents of radicalisation, austerity, othering, and discrimination, but collaboratively write, work and speak up against them from diversified positionalities, from multiple, and contingent perspectives.

Secondly, relating to previous long-term fieldwork with street communities in Indonesia, I would like to highlight that writing with culture, but against xenophobia and exploitation might work best if done in diversified writing and research teams. Over almost fifteen years, I have engaged with communities at the urban margins in teams, never alone. In Indonesia, this ethnographic teamwork managed to counter the politicised public discourse that has for decades constructed the social elites of the Javanese aristocracy as the culturally hegemonic representation of good and primordial citizens. Through a team of diversified collaborators, we took on Javanese anthropology that had for decades idealised the values and ideas of elitist interlocutors during fieldwork in modern anthropology. As wonderful as Clifford Geertz' contributions to anthropological theory are, the protagonist of interpretive anthropology has discursively contributed to the othering of marginalised communities who did not match with these privileged accounts of being ›a good Javanese‹. We took a different perspective and shed light on the perspectives of subaltern and marginalised communities instead of cultural and political elites. We argued that stigmatised and marginalised persons and communities are not deviant per se, but they are first and foremost Javanese and Indonesian. We highlighted that they are also cultural beings, and not so much society's shameful other that needed to be eradicated. So, final sentence to a very long answer: Working through and diversifying the public discourse on culture became a powerful strategy of resistance for stigmatised communities living at the urban margins when they started claiming culture and humanity for themselves publicly.

Birgitt Röttger-Rössler: Thank you very much, Thomas. I think it is very important that you pointed to the potency of resistance to hegemonic discourses via the concept of culture. In my own current work with migrants from Vietnam, I have often observed that they try to resist expectations of assimilation by emphasising their cultural otherness. They insist that ›their culture‹ is very different from what they perceive as the ›German culture‹. Belonging and non-belonging is, as you said, often negotiated by various actors through the concept of culture. We may come back to this point later.

But first, I would like to ask Monique about her opinion. Monique, you emphasise in your work a practice-theoretical approach as well as the bodily dimension of the social. And culture, you argue, is a dimension of the social and becomes embodied during the socialisation process. This adds not only the cultural or cultured body to our discussion, but also points to the complex relation between culture and society. In my opinion this is a very important and interesting aspect. So, what is culture from your practice-oriented perspective?

Monique Scheer: Thank you for your question, and thank you for the invitation, thank you to the two previous speakers for their fascinating comments. You know, it occurred to me that I do not really write all that much about the culture concept, per se. I have not really given it all that much attention in my research. But I do think about it a lot for my teaching. So, I thought I would talk about it from the perspective of how I teach this concept. And to begin with, I would like to point out that, long before there was any talk of getting rid of the culture concept and feeling awkward and uncomfortable about the word ›culture‹, we were already discussing the term ›Ethnologie‹ in Germany as being problematic in the cultural anthropological disciplines of ›Völkerkunde‹ and ›Volkskunde‹. And, you know, at least in my field in Tübingen, we changed the name of ›Volkskunde‹ to ›Empirische Kulturwissenschaft‹ because we liked the term ›culture‹. We thought it was better than ›Volk‹. And so, I've found that in my teaching I try to discuss this term ›culture‹, the pros and cons. Our fields have a long history of struggling with nationalism, with racism, with social conservativism, since they were tasked with producing a picture of ›the way things used to be‹. The struggle against reactionary forces is, therefore, still very high on our agenda, of course. And so we are very careful to minimise any possibility that, when we are talking about culture, it could be used or instrumentalised in any sort of nationalist way. Thus, we teach our students about this from the very beginning, from the first day of class. We are also struggling against everyday public uses of the word ›culture‹, so we have to teach our students what we, as anthropologists, mean when we talk about culture as opposed to what they have been saying up to now or what they are used to reading in the newspaper. We teach them from the very beginning that there is no such thing as Britishness or Swedishness or Germanness. We teach them that culture is a dimension of the social, not a thing in itself. Wherever there is sociality, wherever there are at least two people communicating and interacting, culture is happening. Culture as a dimension of the social means that it is constantly in flux. It is constantly becoming and changing: culture is a process. It is moving forward and backward and sideways and up and down. The link between the social and the cultural can also be understood in terms of ›symbolic behaviors‹, and its changing quality is that of rules being established and contested or misunderstood. And of course, there is a general understanding of culture as expressions that go beyond the everyday, artistic expression which deepens and/or heightens our understanding of ourselves and our relations with others. And so, you can sort of build a bridge between everyday life and the arts or ›high culture‹. Culture does have something to do with tradition – we still have this concept of tradition in the background, and it does have something to do with tradition in the sense that it is learned, it is passed down. But it is also constantly shifting and changing and transforming. This concept, this process-oriented and open concept of culture might seem to contradict a notion of multiculturalism, of more or less clearly defined cultures (in the plural) existing side by side, of cultural diversity. Our students often ask, ›How can that be if culture is constantly moving and shifting and mixing and changing? How can anybody make a claim to cultural ownership and, by virtue of that, make a complaint about cultural appropriation, for example? How does that work?‹ This is why I think that it is very important to keep the link between the social and the cultural very much in the foreground, because then it always means that culture is happening in social relations where there is a flow of power and you have to consider the power relations. Another common understanding of culture that students bring to the classroom is that it is the opposite of nature. But we teach them that it is not enough to say that culture provides humans with everything that nature does not give them. Because when it comes down to it, of course, culture is naturalised, is transformed into ›nature‹ all the time. And nature is obviously shaped by culture. Our bodies are not natural at all. There is hardly anything of significance about our bodies that could be considered natural. Anything that we have in our bodies and on our bodies has been shaped and accentuated, built up or maybe repressed and atrophied, forgotten about through cultural practices. So, something that seems to be as closely tied to the body as, for example, gender is the result of cultural practice. This is a contribution of practice theory, because of course, from that point of view, gender is more or less nothing but practice. And also, the notion of race as a social construct is, I think, very much linked to this kind of thinking of these supposedly bodily features being actually the product of doing, of performing a social and cultural practice. So, an understanding of how culture sort of gets under your skin until it feels natural, as Marcel Mauss (1973) would say, means that you cannot study cultural diversity without looking at bodies and emotions and affects and gestures and comportments and postures and that sort of thing.

So, my last point is about how I have gotten really used to thinking of culture as just being habit. And it is not just because I am interested in the habitus concept. I have been reading a lot of William James in the course of my work on emotions. And he also talks about habit in the *Principles of Psychology* (1910). He discusses the way that humans are creatures of habit, whereas animals are creatures of instinct. And the difference, he says, between humans and animals is that having habits mean you can change them. Even though, of course, it is hard to do so. James also acknowledges that habituation can run very deep, and it can actually enter the materiality of the body and of the brain. One hundred years before modern neuroscience was beginning, James was talking about the plasticity of the brain and how its very materiality is shaped by repetitive behaviors. So culture and cultural practice get under your skin, get into your brain, and feel biological. And therefore it is very hard to tell the difference between behaviors that might be viewed by some psychologists as hardwired or genetically transmitted and those that are habituated to the point of being automated. This is what culture, I think, delivers. It delivers a great deal of these sorts of habits you do not realise that you have. This is what anthropologists find out about people, the habits of behavior and work that they have never thought about before, until they are asked. ›You know, this is how we do this. It is always done this way.‹ There are also habits of thought and feeling. This has been the focus of my work in the history of emotions, to think of emotions as habits and therefore as cultural practices. That might mean you think of a certain person as such and such, because that is just the way the world is. You are just used to thinking of it and feeling about it that way. And because it is in your body, it is not easy to lose this habit, you cannot just willingly stop it happening. Which means, in a sense, it is not really you anyway. Thinking and feeling and doing these things is your habit working through you. It is the culture sort of flowing through you. So, when a group changes their habits of interaction, that is when we start talking about cultural change. And you know, if you can change culture, if you can change habits, then they are not carved in stone. They are the subject of negotiation, they become subject to evaluation. Because then you start thinking: Is this the culture we want to have, or is this something that we should be trying to change? Also thinking about my work at the university, trying to push forward some sort of diversity politics, this becomes an incredibly difficult question. How do you change a culture? We do not have a grip on that, because we do not know that much about how to change habits. But I think it is an important thing to think about when you are trying to achieve certain political goals that involve cultural change. So that is my statement on the topic of culture. I guess I am in between the two of you. I am not against it. I am not particularly in love with it, but I am thinking of it more in terms of ›habits‹ than anything else.

Birgitt Röttger-Rössler: Thank you, Monique, for your comments. I find it very helpful that you have focused attention on how we explain the concept of culture in teaching. We can't just remain vague, we have to be concrete. I myself like to work with a cognitive anthropological concept of culture, according to which culture is defined as knowledge that is learned and shared and that people use to generate behavior and interpret experience. However, this shared knowledge is by no means only explicit knowledge to which individuals have conscious access; rather, a large part of this shared knowledge is of an implicit nature, such as body knowledge, bodylects, all the everyday routines or habits that people acquire in the course of their socialisation. What is important in this understanding of culture as knowledge is to realise that knowledge is shared in multiple and variously complex ways and that no-one ever knows everything – think only of expert knowledge – but that there is a pool of shared knowledge components that allows those who have access to this pool to interact with each other as matter of course. This concept also implies a highly dynamic understanding of culture: knowledge is flexible, it is constantly changing, being expanded, forgotten, useless, and so on. In my opinion, this concept of culture could prove particularly fruitful in relation to heterogeneous, superdiverse social contexts. I wonder what you think of this rather classical concept?

Thomas Stodulka: We talked about culture as an adjective, and it has been around for about 100 plus years as a noun. But actually, we all know it is a verb, right? Culture is relating, practicing, contesting, and imagining, to mention but a few verbs.

Boris Nieswand: The struggle over certain terms can lead astray. In my opinion, it would be intellectualist foolishness to assume that the phenomena addressed by the anthropological concept of culture that you, Birgitt and Thomas, have identified are not important. Of course, there are more or less shared repertoires of knowledge and these, along with the complications you mention, can be subsumed under a processual concept of culture. With my initial reference to Reckwitz I even wanted to indicate that most of us are culturalists in one way or the other. However, if the debates about the political implication of a term, which I have mentioned before, make it more difficult to communicate because the term evokes resistances, I see little use in holding on to it if there are alternatives. These alternatives will probably also be deconstructed and discredited after a while and academics will move on to other concepts. But maybe it is our culture after all, to consume concepts and throw them overboard after a while… In any case it remains important to distinguish between concepts of analysis and concepts of practice, as Rogers Brubaker (2002) calls them. If the people who are in the focus of our research use the concept of culture and when it's relevant to them, it has to be addressed, independent of how I personally think about it. However, this is a different discussion than the question of whether scholars need an analytical concept or a theory of culture. It is possible to study other people's understandings of culture without affirming the concept myself.

Monique Scheer: I fully agree that we have to make this distinction, and this is why I was talking about how you discuss this with students because for them, you have to make a distinction between the way the word ›culture‹ is being used in the world and the way that we are using it in our scholarship. As Boris said, perhaps, you know, as experts on ›culture‹, it would be very wrong not to attend to the ways that the term ›culture‹ is implemented in the real world. And what Thomas pointed out was the way that the term ›culture‹ can become a resource. It can really become a powerful resource for marginalised communities to make a claim that has to be recognised because we have the sense that there's this sort of general consensus that culture is supposed to be respected. I think it's for the same reason that culture and religion get mixed together very often in everyday language: We definitely have a strong, deeply rooted sense that in liberal democratic societies, there must be respect of people's right to religion. And that sort of spills over into their right to ›have a culture‹. And so, if you can say something is your culture, then that is a resource because you can claim it is your human right, and it gives you access to power in negotiations.

Birgitt Röttger-Rössler: My next question goes to Monique because she, in one of her most recent writings, addressed a very important question. Namely, how diversity as a characteristic of society enters into bodies and how it gets incorporated. In other words, Monique asks, I quote her again, »Is there a multicultural body? If so, what might its signature affects and emotions be?«

Monique Scheer: The article you are referring to was really just a little think piece with the title »How does diversity make us feel?« (2020), which was purposefully stated in an ambivalent sense, because I did want to explore whether there might be something like an emotional regime of multicultural societies. Cities that have populations from all over the world moving around sort of put demands on people, and there is an implicit sort of understanding of how you are supposed to feel about it. You're expected to acquire a ›multicultural body‹ in the sense that the demand of this multicultural society is to adapt your affects and your reflexes to being very relaxed about difference, which I called ›multicultural cool‹ in the article. For example, you learn not to stare at someone's hijab while they are talking to you. You learn not to feel annoyed because someone is speaking with a foreign accent. You are being asked to learn these things. And that was the point of the article, which, of course, is totally up for debate. It might be very controversial to make this sort of observation.

Birgitt Röttger-Rössler: Thank you, Monique, these are really important considerations, but doesn't the notion of a multicultural body on the other hand imply that there exists a culturally homogeneous body, which might have particular problems living in culturally diverse settings?

However, this point relates to my second question to Thomas. Thomas, you did classical ethnographic fieldwork based on participant observations in Indonesia; long periods of empirical research in mostly unknown or unfamiliar surroundings and in close daily contact to local people is the trademark of our discipline, and fieldworkers very often characterise their fieldstays as a form of ›second socialization‹. Would you say that emotional repertoires, as well as the sensory capacities of ethnographers, change during fieldwork? Do ethnographers develop multicultural bodies or multicultural emotion repertoires?

Thomas Stodulka: Actually, I do think that. In fieldwork, you do not have all of that embodied, cultural and emotional repertoire advice of attuning to initially unfamiliar lifeworlds provided to you by a textbook or field manual. And I think getting out of your comfort zone in a responsible way can be an important social and political experience because it diversifies your perspectives on what you consider ›normal‹, because you have that scientific aim to ultimately relate to and understand the culturally unfamiliar. And understanding does not work without feeling. In fieldwork you have to learn to position your body differently in order to approach people and places and make friends, it is this harmonising utopia where you put every effort into just ›blending in‹. And until you feel that you can blend into unfamiliar situations, it is a hell of an effort, emotion-wise. It takes quite an emotional effort to not make mistakes all the time. As a consequence, when I returned from Indonesia after five years of intermittent fieldwork, I think my body posture changed because you are not supposed to stand taller or sit higher than someone else. I probably also adjusted my voice very differently in order not to offend anyone. Hanging yourself out in unfamiliar places does something to both body and mind, and everything in-between. And I am not talking about experienced violence or sexual harassment that is often experienced by women anthropologists, my examples refer to very mundane situations and the effects of everyday habituations.

Birgitt Röttger-Rössler: Thank you, Thomas. I think it is important to keep in mind that understanding and knowledge are always connected to our body, are always a bodily practice, particularly when it comes to what we call deep understanding. And understanding never goes without emotions and affects. Our emotions in certain social situations deeply impact how we perceive, interpret and react to what is going on and how we later describe and document it in our anthropological textbooks. In other words, emotions are always evaluative, they often constitute moral assessments in relation to particular social events.

This leads over to my last question to Boris. Boris, in a recent paper, you propose an analytical framework for studying and theorising moral dimensions of representations of migrants and migration in the social sciences (Nieswand 2021). And you argue that it is necessary to critically reflect the often implicit moral attitudes within the writings of migration sociologists. You point to the fact that for many social scientists, integration is positively connoted and constitutes a kind of ›hyper-good‹ as you frame it. They are always emotionally charged. So, in my opinion, you address here also the researchers' affects without saying it, don't you?

Boris Nieswand: Yes, I certainly do. And I also have my own moral agenda when I argue like this. I am concerned, as probably others are, about how the polarisation along issues of migration and diversity will play out in the longer run and how we should deal with it. At least since Trump, I have realised that academia does not hold an ideologically neutral position. It is ultimately committed to a liberal discourse ethic that affirms, for example, pluralism of opinion and is based on the hope that good arguments can prevail over bad ones. In the darkening social atmosphere, in which authoritarianism seems to be on the rise even in countries that thought themselves immune to it, these axioms no longer seem self-evident. I think that polarisation reinforces authoritarian tendencies and thus threatens the social foundations of academic discourse. Some believe that we can counter polarisation through more and better information and political education. I am skeptical in this regard. When it comes to moral affects and moral ways of reasoning, people, myself included, tend to resist information that suggests something other than what we feel is right. Civic education does not work when somebody has the impression that I am not the problem, but the society around me is. Perhaps, and this is my suggestion, what we need is not more facts and more efforts to ›educate the ignorant‹, but rather a reflexive moral sociology of migration and diversity that helps us better understand the social dynamics of different moral ways of feeling and thinking about diversity. Such an endeavor, however, can only be credible if it distances itself from a moral critique that attributes morality to the dumb and uneducated and represents itself as the voice of reason, ethics and enlightenment. In my opinion, such an enterprise can only work if it is relativistic and includes the moral positioning of researchers into its reflexive considerations.

Monique Scheer: I absolutely agree, and this is precisely why I think it is important that we also consider the theory of emotions that underpin our moral sense. If emotions are cultural practices or habits, then some of them can be really stupid, can support very questionable moral positions. And it is important to acknowledge that and try to change them. But we also have a deeply ingrained ideology, which partly comes from science, that emotions are not just habits, but that they are hardwired, that they are natural, and that there is therefore something ›truthy‹ about them. And this is, I think, the source of a lot of the emotional upheaval that we are experiencing: people are taught to listen to their emotions, to pay attention to them, to believe they are saying something true. A lot of people said about right-wing populists: this is just how they feel, we have to take their fears seriously and so on. And I think that we need to take a stand and say emotions are just as cultural as everything else, and they can be just as wrong as a lot of other cultural things. And we should consider what we want to change about them, number one, and secondly, to be less polemic and more anthropological. We could take this stance that Boris was referring to, to reflect on different moral habits of feeling, including our own as scholars, to take all of our schooling in getting to understand the logic of the emotional practices that we are confronted with without assenting to them, without saying they are somehow true or right. I think that our fields are very good at that and can provide tools for this kind of analysis, hopefully instigating change.

Röttger-Rössler: Thank you very much for this thought-provoking conversation. We have addressed numerous aspects that are highly relevant when it comes to sharpening our understanding of the concept of culture. It's particularly telling that emotional and affective factors played a big role in our debate; whether it's Monique's argument that we should think of emotions as habits, that is as the product of cultural practices or the question she raises about the emotional regimes of multicultural societies; be it the discomfort Boris expresses about the concept of culture and the moral affects he mentions, which play an important role in popular as well as academic discourses on migration and diversity; be it the affective efforts Thomas refers to, which are connected with the adaptation of field researchers, but – I would add here – also of migrants to unfamiliar life-worlds and emotional regimes. All this nicely confirms the motto of this conference ›Diversity Affects‹ and is thus able to trouble institutions – as well as our disciplines and their core concepts.

Bibliography

Brubaker, Rogers. 2002. »Ethnicity without Groups.« *Archives Européennes de Sociologie. European Journal of Sociology.* 43 (2): 163-189.

James, William. 1910. *Principles of Psychology.* New York: Holt.

Mauss, Maurice. 1973. *Techniques of the Body. Economy and Society.* 2 (1): 70-88.

Nieswand, Boris/Drotbohm, Heike. 2014. »Einleitung: Die reflexive Wende in der Migrationsforschung.« In: *Kultur, Gesellschaft, Migration.* Wiesbaden: Springer Fachmedien. 1-37.

Nieswand, Boris. 2021. »Konturen einer Moralsoziologie oder Migrationsgesellschaft.« *Zeitschrift für Migrationssoziologie.* (1): 75-95.

Reckwitz, Andreas. 2015. *Unscharfe Grenzen: Perspektiven der Kultursoziologie* (2. Auflage 2010). Bielefeld: transcript Verlag.

Röttger-Rössler, Birgitt. 2018. »Multiple Belongings. On the Affective Dimensions of Migration.« *Zeitschrift für Ethnologie.* 143 (2): 237-262.

Scheer, Monique. 2012. »Are Emotions a Kind of Practice (and is That What Makes Them Have a History)? A Bourdieuian Approach to Understanding Emotion.« *History and Theory.* 51 (2): 193-220.

Scheer, Monique. 2020. »How does Diversity Make Us Feel?: Exploring the Emotional Regimes of Multicultural Societies.« In: *Diversities.* Tübingen: Tübinger Vereinigung für Volkskunde e.V. 61-83.

Stodulka, Thomas. 2021. »Methods and the Construction of Knowledge: Fieldwork and Ethnography.« In: Pedersen, Lene / Cligett, Lisa (eds.). *The SAGE Handbook for Cultural Anthropology.* Thousand Oaks: Sage. 85-194.

Stodulka, Thomas. 2017. *Coming of Age on the Streets of Java – Coping with Marginality, Stigma and Illness.* Bielefeld: transcript.

Stolcke, Verena. 1995. »Talking Culture: New Boundaries, New Rhetorics of Exclusion in Europe.« *Current Anthropology.* 36 (1): 1-24.

Dominika Cohn

Choreografien des Taktilen

Berühren und Berührtwerden als (absente) ästhetische Praxis

ABSTRACT: Bis zum Ausbruch der Corona-Pandemie zeichnete sich in den vergangenen Jahren im zeitgenössischen Tanz – wie in den darstellenden und bildenden Künsten insgesamt – ein Trend hin zu partizipativen Arbeiten ab, bei denen das Publikum sich im Rahmen der Aufführung durch den Raum bewegt und physisch mit Performer*innen und Objekten interagiert. Namhafte Choreograf*innen, darunter William Forsythe, Tino Sehgal oder das Kollektiv Ligna, bezogen ihr Publikum in choreografischen Installationen, Audio-Performances oder ›konstruierten Situationen‹ soweit ins Geschehen ein, dass die Teilnehmenden selbst – ihre Handlungen und Bewegungen – zur eigentlichen Choreografie werden. Doch wie lassen sich solche physischen Formen der Publikumspartizipation rezeptionsästhetisch beschreiben? Dieser Frage nähert sich der Beitrag anhand eines wenig bekannten praktischen Beispiels aus dem Bereich der zeitgenössischen Choreografie, der Arbeit CO-TOUCH der drei russischen Künstlerinnen Kristina Petrova, Katia Reshetnikova und Vera Shchelkina. Mit einem Fokus auf sich im Rahmen dieser Arbeit ereignende Berührungen zwischen Teilnehmer*innen und Performer*innen wird zunächst erläutert, warum sich die hier stattfindende taktile Partizipation als eine Form von Rezeption verstehen lässt. In einem zweiten Schritt wird ein Verständnis von Berührungs-Rezeption als ästhetischer Praxis stark gemacht. Abschließend werden die gewonnenen Erkenntnisse vor der Folie der Pandemie-Geschehnisse reflektiert.

KEYWORDS: Taktilität, Choreografie, Rezeption, Partizipation, ästhetische Praxis

1. Taktile Teilhabe als korporal-sensuelle Partizipation

Hellerau im Januar 2020: Nach anfänglichen Instruktionen durch eine junge Performerin sowie kollektivem Schuhe-Ausziehen vor der Tür wird eine kleine Gruppe Teilnehmer*innen – etwa zehn Menschen gemischten Alters – in einen großen, leeren Saal geführt. An einer Längswand des Saals stehen Stühle aufgereiht, exakt so viele, wie Teilnehmer*innen in den Raum geführt werden.[1] Auf jedem Stuhl liegt ein Kopfhörer

---

[1]   Während dieser einführenden Instruktionen erklärt die Performerin, dass die Performance mit verbundenen Augen stattfinde, für die Sicherheit aller Teilnehmenden aber gesorgt sei. Sie gibt einige praktische Hinweise, z.B. wie mit Brillen zu verfahren sei, dass man bitte die Schuhe ausziehen möge etc. Sie verweist außerdem auf die Möglichkeit, mögliches Unwohlsein jederzeit

Abb. 1: Szene aus CO-TOUCH. Foto: Evgeny Vtorov

bereit. Nach Platznehmen auf einem der Stühle wird den Teilnehmer*innen eine Augenbinde angelegt und der jeweilige Kopfhörer aufgesetzt (oder sie legen sich beides selbst an, dies konnte individuell gewählt werden). Es handelt sich um eine ›Aufführung‹ der partizipativen Choreografie CO-TOUCH, die im Europäischen Zentrum der Künste Hellerau im Rahmen des Festivals ›Karussell – Zeitgenössische Positionen russischer Kunst‹ gezeigt wurde.[2]

Das Spezifikum bei CO-TOUCH ist, dass die Teilnahme mit verbundenen Augen stattfindet. Um sich rezeptionsästhetisch einer Aufführung ohne Sichtbarkeit zu nähern, erscheint es methodisch sinnvoll, die Analyse auf einen persönlichen Erfahrungsbericht zu stützen, der die persönlichen Eindrücke der Autorin während einer

---

     zu signalisieren oder zu äußern. Die Einführung erscheint weichenstellend dafür, dass ich mich als Teilnehmerin willkommen und sicher fühle und sich die Bereitschaft einstellt, mich auf die ›blinde‹ Erfahrung einzulassen.

2   Die drei Künstlerinnen Kristina Petrova, Katia Reshetnikova und Vera Shchelkina arbeiten interdisziplinär zwischen Performance, Tanz, Bewegungsforschung und Sound Art. Vgl.: https://www.hellerau.org/de/event/co-touch/ (letzter Zugriff: 01.10.21). Der Begriff der Choreografie ist in diesem Beitrag weit gefasst und umfasst auch Arbeiten, die sich an der Schnittstelle zu Performance Art, Rauminstallation etc. verorten.

Aufführung von CO-TOUCH schildert.[3] Die Beschreibungsperspektive ist bewusst so gewählt, dass sie der hochgradig subjektiven Wahrnehmung der Geschehnisse Rechnung trägt. Die Verwendung der ich-Perspektive erscheint infolgedessen als die einzig konsequente. Im Folgenden soll ein Auszug aus besagtem Erfahrungsbericht wiedergegeben werden.

Eine Frauenstimme sagt: »breathe in… breathe out… imagine the cerebrospinal fluid running through your spine.« Eine Klangcollage wirkt auf mich ein, während ich gleichzeitig versuche, den Raum um mich herum wahrzunehmen. Irgendwie scheinen die Stühle ganz eng aneinandergerückt oder noch Stühle zwischen die stehenden Stühle geschoben zu werden, jedenfalls spüre ich rechts und links von mir nun andere, sehr dicht bei mir sitzende Körper, spüre deren Unterarme und Körperseiten, die mit meinen in Kontakt sind. Dann fühle ich plötzlich einen ersten ganz direkten Kontakt an meinen Händen: Zwei fremde Hände berühren meine. Sie sind kühl und etwas feucht, berühren mich sehr zart, vermitteln bei der ersten Berührung einen Eindruck von großer Feinfühligkeit – wobei hier der Begriff des Eindrucks durchweg wörtlich zu verstehen ist: Über den feinsten Druck, den die fremden Fingerkuppen auf meine eigenen ausüben, versuche ich mir ein Bild der Person zu machen, die mir nun mit ihren Händen signalisiert, aufzustehen und ein paar Schritte in den Raum hinein zu machen. Dann sind die Berührungen schon wieder verschwunden. Ich stehe und lausche den Geräuschen im Kopfhörer – jetzt auch Vogelzwitschern, Naturgeräusche und Stimmen –, die mal auf Russisch, mal auf Englisch sprechen. Ich fühle, dass ich etwas schwanke, es ist ungewohnt, mit geschlossenen Augen in einem unbekannten Raum zu stehen, zumal sich eigentlich zwei Räume überlappen: der, in dem ich tatsächlich physisch stehe und den ich eben beim Hereinkommen kurz gesehen habe und der, der durch die Klangwelt erzeugt wird, die sich ständig wieder ändert, etwas konfus ist, ohne lineares Zeitgeschehen. Ich fühle mich, als wäre ich schlaftrunken nach ewiger Fahrt aus einem Nachtzug ausgestiegen, an einem fremden Ort, an dem ich keinerlei Orientierung habe. Noch während ich überlege, ob ich mich nun auf eigene Faust in diesen Raum hineinwagen soll, bekomme ich wieder dieselben kühlen, leicht feuchten und zarten Hände zu fühlen – und ich spüre so etwas wie Erleichterung darüber. Sie passt auf mich auf, ›meine‹ Performerin, sie ist da um mich zu leiten. Ich gelange zu dem Schluss, dass ich mich hier gewissermaßen in feste Hände begeben habe: Ein und dieselbe Performerin wird mich berühren und durch Raum und Geschehen leiten. Sie berührt mich nun an verschiedenen Stellen meines Körpers, zunächst sehr vorsichtig, dann auch etwas fester und spielerischer. Sie hat einen angenehmen Händedruck und einen nur ganz fein

---

3   Der Aufführungsbesuch fand am 18.01.2020 um 18:30 Uhr in Hellerau statt. Der Erfahrungsbericht basiert auf Notizen, die unmittelbar nach der Teilnahme von der Autorin angefertigt wurden.

wahrnehmbaren, angenehmen Körpergeruch, den ich als dezent ›öko‹ (irgendwie un-chemisch, nach Naturseife und Wolle) einstufe. Doch warum sollte ich mich nur passiv berühren lassen? Ganz vorsichtig versuche ich, die Berührungen in eigene Bewegungen zu transferieren, hebe langsam den rechten Unterarm, den sie berührt, strecke ihn bis über den Kopf, wir beginnen eine zaghafte gemeinsame Erkundung.

Wie ist diese Szene zu verorten? Eine Performance, während der sich das ›Publikum‹ mit verbundenen Augen in einem Raum befindet, Klangfragmente und Stimmengewirr über Kopfhörer hört, Berührungen empfängt und gleichzeitig und unausweichlich dabei andere berührt. In der Textpassage werden haptische, auditive und olfaktorische Eindrücke, Berührungsempfindungen und Befindlichkeiten geschildert. Kann man in Anbetracht dieser Palette subjektiv-körperlicher, um nicht zu sagen *privater* Eindrücke hier von einer Aufführung mit dem dazugehörigen Publikum sprechen? Ist das über-haupt Kunst (e.g. Choreografie, Performance) oder doch eher eine Art Selbsterfah-rungsworkshop? Diese Fragen lassen sich angesichts der verwirrenden Gemengelage des beschriebenen Geschehens nicht leicht beantworten. Will man sich dem Gegen-stand des Beispiels CO-TOUCH nähern, so scheint hingegen ein anderer Aspekt deutlich hervorzutreten: Ganz offenkundig handelt es sich hier um ein partizipatives Geschehen in einem künstlerischen Kontext.[4] Als Teilnehmerin von CO-TOUCH empfange ich Berührungen, bewege mich durch den Raum und führe meinerseits Berührungen aus, ohne dabei sehen zu können.[5] Ich bin ganz wörtlich mit Haut und Haar im choreografischen Geschehen drin, oder vielmehr: Ich bin zu einem großen Teil selbst das choreografische Geschehen.[6] Die ›Aufführung‹, die ich erlebe, tritt erst durch mein aktives Zutun (das Bewegen durch den Raum und das Empfangen von Berührung mit der Haut meines Körpers) in Existenz. Es gibt nichts zu sehen, es gibt nur Mit-machen: Man partizipiert.

Der Begriff der Partizipation bedarf dabei allerdings genauerer Erläuterungen. Partizipation leitet sich aus dem Lateinischen *participare* für »teilnehmen, teilhaben« ab, das sich wiederum zusammensetzt aus *pars* für »Teil« und *capere* für »nehmen,

---

4   Auf den künstlerischen Kontext weisen sowohl der Veranstaltungsort Hellerau als auch die Bezeichnung des Festivals als »zeitgenössische Positionen russischer Kunst« eindeutig hin.
5   Da in einer Aufführungssituation, die mit verbundenen Augen stattfindet, schwerlich von Zu-schauer*innen gesprochen werden kann, verwende ich hier das Wort Teilnehmer*innen.
6   Aufgrund der in der Performance dominanten Parameter von Bewegung/Körpern in Raum und Zeit (teilweise zu Musik) erscheint es gerechtfertigt, die künstlerische Arbeit im Bereich der Choreografie zu verorten, wenngleich die Grenzen zu Performance Art hier fließend sind. Auch die Tatsache, dass die teilnehmenden Performer*innen fast ausschließlich einen professionellen Tanzhintergrund haben, legt die Verwendung des Choreografiebegriffs nahe.

fassen, ergreifen«.[7] In der beschriebenen Szene handelt es sich dabei ganz buchstäblich um eine Teilhabe mit Anfassen, so dass sich hier durchaus von einer »körperlichen Aktivierung« sprechen lässt – mit Kravagna eine der Voraussetzungen für Beteiligung in partizipativer Kunstpraxis.[8] Darüber, was unter ›partizipativer Kunst‹ zu fassen sei, herrscht dabei allerdings Uneinigkeit.[9] In theoretischen Beiträgen zum Begriff der Partizipation in den Künsten lassen sich hierzu im Großen und Ganzen zwei konträre Positionen bestimmen. Einerseits wird Partizipation verstanden als tatsächliche körperliche Teilhabe an einer Aufführung oder sonstigem Kunstgeschehen. Andererseits wird von vielen Theoretiker*innen in der Tradition Rancières bereits das Zuschauen im Theater für sich als aktiver und partizipativer Akt verstanden.[10] Seitz folgend, lassen sich diese beiden Positionen als ›mentale Teilhabe‹ im Sinne einer konstruktivistischen Weltauffassung einerseits und ›performative Teilhabe‹ im Sinne eines praxistheoretischen Verständnisses andererseits unterscheiden.[11] Diese beiden Positionen sollen im Folgenden kurz erörtert werden. Zunächst zu jenem Verständnis von Partizipation als ›mentaler Teilhabe‹, das hier mit Czirak »Partizipation der Blicke« genannt sei.[12] In diesem Verständnis kommt, auf die performativen Künste bezogen, jegliche Anwesenheit von Zuschauer*innen einer Partizipation gleich, unabhängig davon, ob aktive Partizipation von den Künstler*innen konzipiert wurde oder nicht. Gerade im Kontext der Theaterwissenschaft wird häufig darauf verwiesen, dass der Akt der ästhetischen Rezeption als solcher bereits durch Mit-Sehen, Mit-Hören und Mit-Denken gekennzeichnet sei. Roselt umschreibt dies mit Rückbezug auf Waldenfels etwa mit dem Begriff der Responsivität.[13] Diese Positionen orientieren sich an Rancière, der das (Zu-)Sehen als eigenständige und emanzipatorische Handlung beschreibt: »Die Emanzipation beginnt dann, wenn man den Gegensatz zwischen Sehen und Handeln in Frage stellt

---

7   Vgl. Wolfgang Pfeifer et al. (1993): *Etymologisches Wörterbuch des Deutschen*. Eintrag ›partizipieren‹. https://www.dwds.de/wb/etymwb/partizipieren (letzter Zugriff: 20.09.21).

8   Vgl. Christian Kravagna (1999): »Arbeit an der Gemeinschaft. Modelle partizipatorischer Praxis.« Transversal: https://transversal.at/transversal/1204/kravagna/de (letzter Zugriff: 21.09.21).

9   Wenngleich hier der Fokus auf Choreografie liegt, so erscheint die Verwendung des Überbegriffes ›Künste‹ doch dienlich; zum einen, weil die Partizipationsdiskurse in den bildenden und darstellenden Künsten sich sehr ähneln, zum anderen, weil sich just partizipative Kunstprojekte sehr häufig an Schnittstellen zwischen verschiedenen Kunstgattungen verorten bzw. sich jeglicher Verortung entziehen.

10 Vgl. Jacques Rancière (2009): *Der emanzipierte Zuschauer*. Wien: Passagen Verlag.

11 Vgl. Hanne Seitz (2012): »Impulsvortrag Partizipation. Formen der Beteiligung im zeitgenössischen Theater.« http://www.was-geht-berlin.de/sites/default/files/hanne_seitz_partizipation_2012.pdf (letzter Zugriff: 13.05.20).

12 Adam Czirak (2012): *Partizipation der Blicke. Szenerien des Sehens und Gesehenwerdens in Theater und Performance*. Bielefeld: transcript.

13 Vgl. Jens Roselt (2012): Den Augen trauen: Theater und Phänomenologie. In: Fischer-Lichte, Erika/Czirak, Adam/Jost, Torsten et al. (Hg.): *Die Aufführung. Diskurs – Macht – Analyse*. München: Wilhelm Fink, S. 267-269.

[…].«[14] Daraus folgt für Rancière in logischer Konsequenz ein »Verwischen der Grenze zwischen denen, die handeln, und denen, die zusehen […].«[15] Liegt die Zuschauer*innen-Emanzipation dieser Auffassung zufolge darin, dass jede*r seine oder ihre eigene Interpretation machen kann, dann macht dies eine Unterteilung in aktive und (vermeintlich) passive Zuschauer*innen obsolet: Die Anwesenheit einer Zuschauerin im Theater bedeutet nach dieser Auffassung ganz automatisch, dass sie durch ihr Zusehen, Zuhören, Mit-Denken an der Aufführung Teil hat und Teil nimmt.[16]

Wenn jedoch das Zuschauen im Theater für sich als partizipativer Akt verstanden wird, wie lassen sich dann die zahlreichen performativen Formate auf Festivals, in Galerien und Spielstätten fassen, bei denen ganz bewusst mit einem Zuschauen aus der sicheren Distanz des Theatersessels gebrochen wird? Formate, in denen etwa gemeinsam gegessen,[17] durch Schlamm gewatet[18] oder kollektiv im Theater übernachtet wird?[19] Zuschauer*innen werden hier dezidiert aufgefordert, sich bei der jeweiligen künstlerischen Arbeit körperlich zu involvieren, Handlungen auszuführen oder selbst Entscheidungen zu treffen.[20] In der Fachliteratur wird Partizipation in solchen Projekten, wie oben bereits kurz umrissen, als Form tatsächlicher körperlicher Tätigkeit im Sinne einer performativen Publikumsteilhabe verstanden. In diesem Verständnis wird, wie Spohn herausarbeitet, eine »Analogie von Aktivität und physischem Handeln« vorausgesetzt.[21] Dabei wird in partizipativer Kunst vielfach Teilhabe als solche bereits als *per se* politisch verstanden: »Die ›politische Dimension einer partizipativen

---

14   Rancière 2009, S. 23.
15   Vgl. Rancière 2009, S. 30.
16   Vgl. hierzu auch Gerald Siegmund (2016): »Das Problem der Partizipation.« Goethe Institut: https://www.goethe.de/ins/es/de/kul/sup/bew/20708712.html (letzter Zugriff: 21.09.21). Dass im Umkehrschluss eine Aufführung ohne Zuschauer*innen wahrlich nicht dasselbe ist, wie eine Aufführung vor voller Tribüne, hat die Corona-Zeit für Theaterschaffende schmerzlich spürbar gemacht.
17   Z.B. bei Rirkrit Tiravanijas Dinners-Installationen. Vgl. Julia Keller (2021): »From Studio to Dining Table: Rirkrit Tiravanija.« Schirn: https://www.schirn.de/en/magazine/whats_cooking/vom_atelier_an_den_esstisch_rirkrit_tiravanija/ (letzter Zugriff: 11.10.21).
18   So geschah es beispielsweise bei Santiago Sierras »Haus im Schlamm« (2005) in der Kestner Gesellschaft Hannover. Vgl. Wolfgang Kemp (2015): *Der explizite Betrachter.* Konstanz: Konstanz University Press, S. 166ff.
19   Etwa im Projekt »Hotel Berlin« von Stefan Nolte, Ruth Feindel und Paul Brodowsky, dass 2016 im Berliner Ballhaus Ost stattfand. Vgl. https://www.ballhausost.de/produktionen/hotel-berlin/ (letzter Zugriff: 11.10.21).
20   Für eine umfassende Kompilation und Analyse partizipativer Kunstformate vgl. Silke Feldhoff (2009): »Zwischen Spiel und Politik: Partizipation als Strategie und Praxis in der bildenden Kunst.« https://opus4.kobv.de/opus4-udk/frontdoor/deliver/index/docId/26/file/Feldhoff_Silke.pdf (letzter Zugriff: 20.09.21).
21   Anna Spohn (2016): Die Idee der Partizipation und der Begriff der Praxis. In: Kauppert, Michael/Eberl, Heidrun (Hg.): *Ästhetische Praxis.* Berlin: Springer VS, S. 43.

Kunst‹«, so Spohn, »scheint somit alleine der Teilnahme, einer nach außen sichtbaren Beteiligung, geschuldet.« Differenziert benennt Claire Bishop in ihrem umfangreichen Werk zu Partizipation in der Kunst als deren zentrale Dimensionen emanzipatorische ›Ermächtigung‹ der Zuschauer*innen, die Auseinandersetzung mit Fragen der Autor*innenschaft sowie Gemeinschaft.[22] Dabei sind partizipative künstlerische Formate durch Bishop und diverse andere Autor*innen starker Kritik ausgesetzt. Relevante Kritikpunkte sind etwa, dass die performative Teilhabe an einem Kunstgeschehen durch mangelnde Distanz ein ›wahres‹ ästhetisches Erleben behindere,[23] dass faktisch bestehende Hierarchien im Sinne einer angestrebten ›Gleichheit aller‹ verwischt würden[24] und dass die Projekte vielfach zu wirtschaftlichen Zwecken instrumentalisiert würden, etwa um Audience Development zu betreiben.[25]

An dieser Stelle zurück zu CO-TOUCH. Auch hier wird mit dem Vom-Zuschauersessel-aus-Zusehen gebrochen, sogar gleich zweifach: Denn einerseits sitzt hier niemand in einem Zuschauersessel und anderseits schaut niemand zu, weil allen Teilnehmer*innen die Augen verbunden sind.[26] Da es nichts zu sehen gibt, stellt die direkte körperliche Involvierung qua Hautkontaktes und eigenen Bewegens hier offenbar das künstlerische Programm dar. Damit scheint keine der beiden oben umrissenen Positionen zu Partizipation das hier vorgestellte Beispiel angemessen zu fassen. Einerseits geht das Berühren, Berührt-Werden und gemeinsame Bewegen weit über eine Partizipation im Sinne eines rein intellektuellen Mit-Denkens hinaus. Anderseits lässt sich das blinde Durch-den-Raum-Tapsen zwar mit Kravagna durchaus als eine Form der Zuschauer*innen-Aktivierung bezeichnen, entzieht sich jedoch, zumindest auf den ersten Blick, der damit verbundenen Logik des Partizipierens als dezidiert politischem Akt.[27] Vielmehr scheint hier Berührung gleichzeitig künstlerisches Mittel und künst-

---

22   Claire Bishop (2006): *Participation. Documents of Contemporary Art*. London: MIT Press, S. 12.

23   Vgl. Kai van Eikels (2019): »Vorlesungsscript ›Partizipation. Ansprüche und Wirklichkeiten des Politischen in den Künsten‹.« Die Kunst des Kollektiven: https://kunstdeskollektiven.wordpress.com/2019/02/08/vorlesungsmanuskript-partizipation-ansprueche-und-wirklichkeiten-des-poli tischen-in-den-kuensten/ (letzter Zugriff: 21.09.21).

24   Vgl. Siegmund 2016: »Partizipation verspricht Gleichheit, die jedoch auch in einer offenen Aufführungssituation nicht einfach herzustellen ist. Schließlich gibt es immer eine Gruppe von Künstlern, die sich die Situation ausgedacht und die Spielregeln festgelegt hat, denen die Zuschauer folgen sollen.« Vgl. zu diesem Aspekt auch Seitz 2012, S. 9.

25   Vgl. Seitz 2012, S. 9/10.

26   Die Performer*innen selbst können zwar sehen und sind damit sicherlich ein stückweit ›Zuschauer*innen‹, aber eben innerhalb ihrer Rolle als Ausführende der Berührungen und die Teilnehmer*innen Begleitende.

27   Gleichwohl stellt sich die Frage, ob nicht die Bereitschaft, sich auf das Berührungsgeschehen einzulassen bzw. dieses möglicherweise auch zu verweigern, durchaus eine politische Dimension beinhaltet. Ich beziehe mich hier aber zunächst auf die im Partizipationsdiskurs häufig stattfindende polemische Gleichsetzung von physischem Mitmachen als einem politischen Tun

lerischer Zweck: Petrova, Reshetnikova und Shchelkina erschaffen mit CO-TOUCH ein choreografisches Dispositiv, in welchem durch gezielte Ausschaltung des Sehsinns eine Fokussierung auf Berührungswahrnehmungen stattfindet.[28] Die im Beispiel CO-TOUCH stattfindende Rezeption lässt sich, so mein Vorschlag, mit einem korporal-sensuellen Partizipationsbegriff fassen, welcher eine dezidierte Betonung auf Körper- bzw. Sinneswahrnehmung setzt. Hierfür schlage ich folgende Definition vor: Von korporal-sensueller Partizipation lässt sich dann sprechen, wenn sich verschiedene durch eine choreografische (e.g. künstlerische) Arbeit aktivierte sensuelle Wahrneh-mungen erst durch und mit einer körperlichen Teilhabe des ›Publikums‹ entfalten können: Haut kann, wie bei CO-TOUCH, erst dann fühlen, wenn sie tatsächlich berührt oder berührt wird. Dabei will ich, Seitz folgend, dafür plädieren, korporal-sensuelle Partizipation wie das Berühren im hier ausgewählten Beispiel als einen spezifischen Modus von *Rezeption* zu verstehen, mit und in dem ich als teilnehmende Zuschauerin einer bestimmten Performance in einem bestimmten Moment begegne.[29] Um diesen Vorschlag nachvollziehbar zu machen, werde ich etwas ausholen und die Diskurse zu Rezeptionsästhetik und der sogenannten Relationalen Ästhetik streifen, um dabei insbesondere die Rolle der Rezipient*innen in den Blick zu nehmen. Vor diesem Hin-tergrund werde ich dann ein Verständnis von Berührungs-Rezeption als ästhetischer Praxis stark machen, die ein Gegenmodell zur gängigen Sinneshierarchie darstellt. Abschließend werde ich die gewonnenen Erkenntnisse vor dem Hintergrund der ak-tuellen Pandemie-Situation reflektieren.

2. Rezeption von Berührung im partizipativ-choreografischen Rahmen

Zunächst zur Rezeptionsästhetik: Aufs Gröbste vereinfacht, handelt es sich dabei um die Wissenschaft, die nach Wahrnehmungen einer literarischen oder künstlerischen Arbeit durch die Leser*innen bzw. Betrachter*innen fragt. Sie richtet also ihr Augen-merk auf die Position des- oder derjenigen, die ein Kunstwerk wahrnimmt, und damit gleichzeitig auf den Akt der Wahrnehmung als solchen. Während traditionell der

---

per se, mit dem sich, so will ich behaupten, die taktile Partizipation in CO-TOUCH nicht ausreichend fassen lässt. Dennoch entfaltet die Arbeit in ihrer Betonung des Taktilen durchaus ein relevantes politisches Potential, auf das ich an späterer Stelle noch eingehen werde.

28 Auch akustische Wahrnehmung spielt eine sehr große Rolle bei CO-TOUCH; diese scheint durch ihren fragmentierten Charakter jedoch stark zu dem Zweck eingesetzt, ein diffuses Raumgefühl zu schaffen bzw. sogar eine gewisse Orientierungslosigkeit hervorzurufen, was wiederum die Konzentration auf den Tastsinn als einzige Orientierungs- und Informationsquelle im tatsächlichen Raum des Geschehens umso stärker betont.

29 Vgl. Seitz 2012, S. 8: Die Autorin schlägt hier ein Verständnis von Partizipation als »besondere Form der Rezeption« vor.

Werksbegriff übergeordnet war – die Frage nach einer ›absoluten‹ Bedeutung des jeweiligen Kunstwerks –, wird, spätestens seitdem Roland Barthes den bekannten ›Tod des Autors‹ proklamiert hat, der Seite der Rezipierenden immer größere Aufmerksamkeit geschenkt.[30] Kemp datiert ganz konkret die »Geburt der Rezeptionsästhetik« auf das Jahr 1967:[31] dem Jahr, in dem sich Vertreter[32] der Konstanzer Schule explizit dem Projekt ›Rezeptionsästhetik‹ zu widmen beginnen und damit der Rolle der Leser*in.[33] Seither gilt, wie Schweppenhäuser festhält: »Das künstlerische Werk oder die Aktion wird erst im Akt der Rezeption durch die Betrachter – oder die Beteiligten – vervollständigt.«[34] Damit wird den sogenannten Beteiligten bzw. dem nun nicht mehr nur zuschauenden Publikum ein ganz neuer Handlungsspielraum zuteil. Kemp schreibt dieser Tatsache eine enorme Bedeutung zu:

> Die Rezeptionsästhetik war insofern der erfolgreichste der geistes-wissenschaftlichen Neuansätze der Nachkriegszeit, als die Größe, auf die sie sich konzentrierte, sehr bald zu einem leeren Signifikanten aufstieg: das Publikum, es konnte mit einem Mal nicht mehr geleugnet werden, es war da und wollte hofiert, erforscht, beschäftigt, unterhalten werden, es war da und es wollte mitreden, es war da und konnte als unübersehbare Größe auch Widerstand und Aggression auslösen […].[35]

Das Publikum war in den Künsten und ihren dazugehörigen Diskursen angekommen – und blieb: geliebt, verhasst, willkommen geheißen und sperrig.

Noch größer wurde die Wirkkraft des Publikums Ende der 1990er Jahre mit der durch Bourriaud begründeten Relationalen Ästhetik – einer, wenn man so will, radikalen Fortentwicklung der Rezeptionsästhetik. Hier geht es nicht mehr um einen Handlungsspielraum, der dem Publikum in der Rezeption der künstlerischen Arbeiten zuteilwird; hier werden die Handlungen zwischen Publikum und Akteur*innen nun selbst zur eigentlichen Kunst. Anstelle von ›Kunstwerken‹ treten durch Künstler*innen gestaltete Situationen, die in wie auch immer gearteter Weise Raum für Begegnung, Interaktion und Handlungen schaffen. »Meetings, encounters, events, various types of collaboration between people, games, festivals, and places of conviviality«, listet Bourriaud auf, »in a word all manner of encounter and relational invention thus

---

30 Vgl. hierzu z.B. Kemp 2015, S. 11.
31 Kemp 2015, S. 9.
32 In diesem Fall waren es tatsächlich nur männlicher Vertreter, zu denen u.a. der Romanist Hans Robert Jauß und der Anglist Wolfgang Iser zählen. Vgl. Kemp 2015, S. 9.
33 Vgl. Kemp 2015, S. 9.
34 Gerhard Schweppenhäuser (2007): *Ästhetik. Philosophische Grundlagen und Schlüsselbegriffe.* Frankfurt am Main: Campus, S. 275.
35 Kemp 2015, S. 50.

represent, today, aesthetic objects likely to be looked at as such [...].«[36] Für Bourriaud selbst stellt dies eine Entwicklung von ebenso historischer Größe dar wie die Entwicklung der Rezeptionsästhetik für Kemp: Relationale Kunst habe, so konstatiert Bourriaud, die althergebrachte Ordnung abgelöst: »After the area of relations between Humankind and deity, and then between Humankind and the object, artistic practice is now focused upon the sphere of inter-human relations [...]«[37] Für den hier gesteckten Fokus soll angemerkt werden, dass Relationaler Kunst mit ihrer Betonung auf Begegnung und Prozess von Kemp ein »anti-okulärer Vorbehalt« zugeschrieben wird;[38] vergleichbar konstatiert auch Bishop eine anti-visuelle Tendenz.[39] Wenn nach dem Verständnis Bourriauds Intersubjektivität in Form von zwischenmenschlichen Beziehungen den Kern künstlerischer Praxis darstellt,[40] dann erscheinen Begriffe wie ›Zuschauer*innen‹ oder ›Betrachter*innen‹ im Zusammenhang mit Relationaler Kunst vollkommen unzulängliche Termini. Bourriaud schlägt stattdessen Begriffe wie »witness, associate, customer, guest, coproducer, and protagonist« vor.[41] Hierin liegt nun im Kern ein enger Zusammenhang zwischen Relationaler Kunst und partizipativer Kunst begründet. Eine Kunstform, deren Rezipient*innen sich als Verbraucher*innen, Co-Produzent*innen oder sogar Protagonist*innen verstehen dürfen, basiert auf deren Teilhabe und ist daher gewissermaßen qua definitonem partizipativ zu nennen. Von Kemp selbst werden die Begriffe ›partizipatorische Kunst‹ und ›relationale Kunst‹ tatsächlich als Synonyme verwendet.[42] Basierend auf dem oben herausgearbeiteten aktiven Rezipient*innen-Verständnis in der Rezeptionsästhetik erscheint es somit gerechtfertigt, korporal-sensuelle Partizipation wie im Beispiel CO-TOUCH als spezifische Form der *Rezeption* zu bezeichnen.

Mit dieser Feststellung springe ich zurück zum Ausgangsbeispiel. Bis hierhin wurde festgestellt, dass das Aufführungsgeschehen bei CO-TOUCH sich erst mittels korporal-sensueller Partizipation der Teilnehmenden entfalten kann und dass diese Partizipation sich als eine spezifische und sehr aktive Form der Rezeption verstehen lässt. Doch was genau bedeutet Rezeption im Falle dieses Beispiels ganz konkret? Diese Frage beinhaltet, genau genommen, eigentlich zwei Fragen, nämlich erstens: *Was* wird hier rezipiert? Und zweitens: *Wie* wird hier rezipiert? Zur Erinnerung: Beschrieben wurde

---

36 Nicolas Bourriaud (2010): *Relational Aesthetics.* Monts: Les presses du réel, S. 28/29.

37 Bourriaud 2010, S. 28.

38 Kemp 2015, S. 154.

39 Vgl. Claire Bishop (2012): *Artificial Hells. Participatory Art and the Politics of Spectatorship.* London/New York: Verso, S. 6.

40 Vgl. Bourriaud 2010, S. 28: »As part of a ›relationist‹ theory of art, inter-subjectivity [...] becomes the quintessence of artistic practice.«

41 Nicolas Bourriaud (Hg.) (2002): *Postproduction. Culture as Screenplay: How Art Reprograms the World.* New York: Sternberg Press, S. 58.

42 Vgl. Kemp 2015, S. 166.

mit dem Beispiel CO-TOUCH eine Aufführungssituation, in der sich ca. 10 Teilnehmende pro Einlassrunde mit verbundenen Augen und Kopfhörern in einem großen Saal befinden. Während der ›Aufführung‹ interagieren Performer*innen mit den Teilnehmenden per Berührung. Damit erscheint CO-TOUCH als eine Art Anti-Spektakel, denn zu sehen ist hier: nichts! Dennoch ist der oben zitierte Auszug des Erfahrungsberichtes reich an Eindrücken, die aufgrund der Ausklammerung jeglicher visuellen Wahrnehmung nunmehr haptisch, kinästhetisch, akustisch und olfaktorisch sind. Wiederholt tauchen Beschreibungen von Berührungserfahrungen in dem exemplarisch ausgewählten Auszug des Erfahrungsberichtes auf, etwa hier:[43] »[…] jedenfalls spüre ich rechts und links von mir nun andere, sehr dicht bei mir sitzende Körper, spüre deren Unterarme und Körperseiten, die mit meinen in Kontakt sind.« Oder, etwas später: »Über den feinsten Druck, den die fremden Fingerkuppen auf meine eigenen ausüben […].« Beschrieben werden Berührungseindrücke unterschiedlicher Qualität: flächiger Körperkontakt und hochpräziser Hautkontakt der Fingerkuppen. Auch die Beschaffenheit der berührenden Körperteile wird in ihren spezifischen Qualitäten beschrieben, beispielsweise in dieser Passage: »Noch während ich überlege, […] bekomme ich wieder dieselben kühlen, leicht feuchten und zarten Hände zu fühlen […]« Die empfangene Berührung stellt dabei eine Form von Kommunikation zwischen mir als Teilnehmerin und den Performer*innen bzw. der Umgebung dar: Stellenweise scheinen sich die Berührungen als Aufforderung deuten zu lassen, etwa wenn von der Person die Rede ist, »die mir nun mit ihren Händen signalisiert, aufzustehen und ein paar Schritte in den Raum hinein zu machen.« Die Möglichkeit, nicht nur Berührung zu empfangen, sondern auch aktiv und eigenständig auf die Berührungen zu reagieren, etwa Schritte in den unbekannten Raum hinein zu wagen, ist hier deutlich angelegt. Zusammenfassend lässt sich als Antwort auf die Frage, *was* im Beispiel CO-TOUCH rezipiert wird, formulieren: Hier wird in erster Linie Berührung rezipiert. Diese Antwort wirkt gewiss zunächst vollkommen banal – zumal sie in Anbetracht des Wortes ›touch‹ im Titel wenig originell anmutet. Die Feststellung zieht jedoch interessante Erkenntnisse nach sich, wenn man die zweite der beiden oben gestellten Fragen hinzuzieht: *Wie* wird hier rezipiert?

Die Rezeption der Berührung findet über die Oberflächen meines Körpers statt, vor allem über die Haut. Wenn das *Was* der Rezeption Berührung darstellt, dann muss das *Wie* der Rezeption der Körper im Modus des Fühlens sein, also fühlend oder empfindend. Damit liegt es nahe, hier in der phänomenologischen Tradition Merleau-Pontys von *leiblicher* Wahrnehmung zu sprechen. Der phänomenologische Leib betont, wie es Bedorf zusammenfasst, den empfindenden »Eigenleib« im Unterschied zum Körper als

---

43 Im hier formulierten Forschungsinteresse sei eine Vernachlässigung anderer nicht-visueller Wahrnehmungseindrücke zugunsten der haptisch-taktilen Momente gerechtfertigt.

einem zergliederbaren und vermeintlich objektivierbaren »Körperding«.[44] Die Körper-
Leib-Unterscheidung beschreibt Bedorf pointiert: »Dieser gelebte Leib, den wir nicht
nur haben, sondern der wir immer stets schon sind, unterscheidet sich insofern vom
objektiven Körperding, als wir nie um ihn herumgehen und ihn entsprechend nie völlig
in den Blick nehmen können.«[45] Der Leib wird so zum »Wahrnehmungsorgan«, zum
»Nullpunkt der Orientierung«, zur »Weise des Weltzugangs«.[46] Mit dem Verweis auf
das phänomenologische Verständnis von ›Leib‹ soll für das Beispiel CO-TOUCH
festgehalten werden, dass die Rezeption von Berührung hier über einen Zustand des
leiblichen In-Berührung-Seins stattfindet. Die in der Performance stattfindende korporal-sensuelle Partizipation lässt sich damit spezifischer als eine *leiblich-taktile Rezeption* fassen. Dabei ist das Wahrnehmen von Berührung untrennbar verquickt mit
Bewegen: Es kann keinen Hautkontakt geben ohne eine Körperbewegung zu diesem
hin. Die Wahrnehmung bei CO-TOUCH geschieht damit über ein aktives Tun im
Prozess. Ich rezipiere Berührungen und Bewegungsimpulse, indem ich hier tatsächlich
›mit Haut und Haar‹ teilnehme und mich selber durch den Raum bewege. Der re-
sponsive Charakter dieser leiblich-taktilen Rezeption soll anhand einer weiteren
Textstelle aufgeführt werden: »Doch warum sollte ich mich nur passiv berühren lassen? Ganz vorsichtig versuche ich, die Berührungen in eigene Bewegungen zu transferieren, hebe langsam den rechten Unterarm, den sie berührt, strecke ihn bis über den
Kopf, wir beginnen eine zaghafte gemeinsame Erkundung.« Im Empfangen einer Be-
wegungsrichtung durch eine berührende Hand, deren Arm in Bewegung ist, liegt
zugleich die Einladung, mich selbst zu bewegen, Bewegung und Berührung zurück-
zugeben, eine eigene Variation zu erfinden. So bleibt der Akt der Berührungsrezeption,
dergestalt als aktiver Prozess verstanden, in seinem Verlauf offen. Mit Schmidt gesprochen beinhaltet er damit immer auch einen gewissen »Eigensinn«.[47]

Nachdem nun etwas genauer auf das *Was* und *Wie* der Rezeption in der choreografischen Arbeit CO-TOUCH eingegangen wurde, lässt sich folgendes Zwischenfazit
ziehen: Die Kommunikation zwischen Teilnehmer*innen und Performer*innen erfolgt
hier ausschließlich über Berührung.[48] Durch die inszenierte Ausschaltung des Sehsinns

---

44 Thomas Bedorf (2015): Leibliche Praxis. Zum Körperbegriff in den Praxistheorien. In: Alke-
     meyer, Thomas/Schürmann, Volker/Volbers, Jörg (Hg.): *Praxis denken. Konzepte und Kritik.*
     Wiesbaden: Springer VS, S. 139. Auf den umfassenden Diskurs zum Begriff der Leiblichkeit kann
     hier aus Gründen des Umfangs nicht weiter eingegangen werden.
45 Bedorf 2015, S. 139.
46 Bedorf 2015, S. 138.
47 Jens Schmidt (2021): Ästhetische Praxis als ökologische Konzeption. Situationen relational-
     divergierender Rezeptionspraxis. In: Corsten, Michael (Hg.): *Praxis. Ausüben. Begreifen.* Wei-
     lerswist: Velbrück Verlag, S. 198.
48 In dieser Hinsicht gibt es sicherlich Überschneidungen von CO-TOUCH mit der Tanzpraxis der
     Contact Improvisation. Auch die Contact Improvisation arbeitet mit einem stetigen Geben und

schafft die Arbeit einen Rahmen, der die Wahrnehmung der Teilnehmenden auf das taktile Geschehen lenkt. Das, was hier als das choreografische Geschehen zu bezeichnen ist, erschließt sich so ausschließlich über das Empfangen und Weitergeben von Berührung in Kombination mit eigener Bewegung. Zugespitzt formuliert: Das Berühren, Berührt-Werden und Bewegen selbst *sind* die eigentliche Choreografie.[49] Deren Rezeption findet physisch aktiv – berührend und bewegend – statt und setzt gleichzeitig einen Prozess des Wahrnehmens eben dieser Berührung und Bewegung in Gang. Um dem dergestalt aktiven, prozesshaften und leiblich-situierten Charakter der hier stattfindenden Rezeption gerecht zu werden, schlage ich vor, diese selbst als ästhetische Praxis zu begreifen.

3. Leiblich-taktile Rezeption als ästhetische Praxis

Um diesen Vorschlag plausibel zu machen, muss zunächst etwas ausgeholt werden. Der Versuch, in einem choreografischen Setting stattfindende Berührungen – Berührungen wohlgemerkt, die dabei nicht sichtbar, sondern ausschließlich fühlbar werden –, als ästhetische Praxis zu beschreiben, entpuppt sich als recht komplexes Unterfangen: Jeder der beiden Begriffe zieht seit der Antike eine lange und sehr kontroverse Theoriegeschichte nach sich, auf die an dieser Stelle nicht eingegangen werden kann und soll. Sinnvoll erscheint jedoch ein gezielter Rückgriff auf den antiken Begriff der Aisthesis. Im Kontext von Aisthesis und Berührung soll außerdem der Begriff des Okularzentrismus vorgestellt werden. Schließlich werden auch einige wesentliche Merk-

---

Nehmen von Bewegung und einer offenen, responsiven Haltung der Praktizierenden, die als ›body listening‹ bezeichnet wird. Allerdings handelt es sich bei der Contact Improvisation um eine Technik, die, wenngleich prinzipiell offen für körperliche Diversität, vor einer Teilnahme an Jams durchaus erst zu einem gewissen Grad zu erlernen ist, z.B. in Workshops. Im Unterschied dazu erfordert die Teilnahme an CO-TOUCH keinerlei Vorerfahrung oder physische Vorbereitung (abgesehen vom Ausziehen der Schuhe). Zum Prinzip des ›listening‹ in der Contact Improvisation vgl. Gabriele Brandstetter (2013): »Listening«. Kinesthetic Awareness in Contemporary Dance, in: dies., Gerko Egert und Sabine Zubarik (Hg.): *Touching and Being Touched. Kinesthesia and Empathy in Dance and Movement.* Berlin/Boston: De Gruyter, S. 163-179.

49 Hierin unterscheidet sich CO-TOUCH schließlich, um meine polemische Frage nach dem »Selbsterfahrungsworkshop« noch einmal aufzugreifen, ganz entscheidend von anderen, nicht-künstlerischen Situationen, in denen Berührung eine Rolle spielt, etwa bei Gesundheitsanwendungen, in therapeutischen oder pädagogischen Formaten. Dort wird Berührung als Mittel zu einem bestimmten Zweck angewendet, während CO-TOUCH einen Raum für ein ästhetisches Wahrnehmen von Bewegung als solcher schafft. Dabei sei nicht ausgeschlossen, dass sich die leiblich-taktile Rezeption einer Arbeit wie CO-TOUCH für Einzelne momentweise mit Erfahrungen aus anderen Berührungssituationen überschneiden mag.

male des Praxisbegriffs vorgestellt, um präzise darstellen zu können, inwiefern leiblich-taktile Rezeption hier als ästhetische Praxis verstanden werden soll.

Im Zusammenhang mit dem Beispiel CO-TOUCH erscheint ein Rückgriff auf die ursprüngliche Wortherkunft des Ästhetikbegriffes weiterführend. Ästhetik leitet sich ab vom griechischen ›Aisthesis‹ für ›Wahrnehmung, Gewahrwerden‹ und bezieht sich in seiner ursprünglichen Wortbedeutung also stark auf die sinnliche Komponente des Wahrnehmens.[50] Hetzel stellt heraus:

> Die Ästhetik versteht sich zunächst als aisthetik, als Wahrnehmungslehre. Sie fragt danach, wie sich Wahrnehmungen von Dingen, die wir als schön bezeichnen, von Wahrnehmungen anderer Phänomene unterscheiden, die wir etwa als wahr oder gut charakterisieren würden.[51]

Damit fungiert Aisthesis, so Hetzel, als »Schlüsselbegriff der Aristotelischen Er-kenntnistheorie, er steht dort für die sinnliche Wahrnehmung als Teil des Erkennt-nisprozesses.«[52] Während für das hier vorgestellte praktische Beispiel die Verwendung der Bezeichnung ›schön‹ zu Ambivalenzen führt und wenig zielführend wirkt, er-scheint die Betonung des Vorgangs der Wahrnehmung in der Aisthesis durchaus weiterführend. Allerdings muss hier auf eine Problematik verwiesen werden, die im Zusammenhang von Aisthesis und Berührung relevant ist. Im antiken Verständnis betont der Begriff der Aisthesis, wie ausgeführt, die sinnliche Wahrnehmung, unter-scheidet dabei aber stark in der Relevanz der unterschiedlichen Sinne bzw. weist den Sinnen sogar eine Art Rangfolge zu. Auf diese Problematik verweist auch Hetzel: »Der Ausgang von der aisthesis bringt die Ästhetik dabei zunächst in eine okularzentristi-sche Schieflage, sie privilegiert den Gesichtssinn gegenüber allen anderen Sinnen.«[53] Um Rezeption im Beispiel CO-TOUCH als ästhetische Praxis beschreiben zu können, erscheint es notwendig, auch den Begriff des Okularzentrismus zu erläutern.

Zur Erklärung des Terminus muss an vorderster Stelle auf die sogenannte ›Hier-archie der Sinne‹ verwiesen werden. Diese basiert auf einer grundsätzlichen Unter-teilung in fünf verschiedene menschliche Sinne, die bereits auf Aristoteles' *De Anima* zurückgeht.[54] Wenngleich Wissenschaftler*innen inzwischen eine Unterteilung in

---

50   Vgl. Bernd Ternes (2000): »Zum Begriff der Wahrnehmung/Aisthesis.« Aisthesis Verlag: https://www.aisthesis.de/epages/63645342.sf/de_DE/?ObjectPath=/Shops/63645342/Categories/AboutUs/Aisthesis/Begriff_Aisthesis (letzter Zugriff: 21.09.21).

51   Andreas Hetzel (2021): Im Vollzug. Praxis als Grundbegriff einer Aristotelischen Ästhetik. In: Corsten, Michael (Hg.): *Praxis. Ausüben. Begreifen.* Weilerswist: Velbrück Verlag, S. 74.

52   Hetzel 2021, S. 74.

53   Hetzel 2021, S. 74.

54   Vgl. Aristoteles (2020): *Über die Seele.* Übersetzt und herausgegeben von Gernot Krapinger. Stuttgart: Reclam. S. 127.

wesentlich mehr Sinne vornehmen,[55] so wird ihre aristotelische Fünfteilung doch auch noch heute in der Regel als gängig betrachtet. Jütte zeigt auf, dass Aristoteles diesen fünf Sinnen eine Art Rangordnung zuschreibt:[56] An oberster Stelle stehe ›visus‹, der Sehsinn oder sogenannte Gesichtssinn, gefolgt von ›auditus‹, dem Gehör. In der Mitte befänden sich ›odoratus‹, der Geruchssinn, und ›gustus‹, der Geschmackssinn. Als ›niedersten‹ Sinn ganz am Ende der Skala nenne Aristoteles ›tactus‹, den Tastsinn.[57] Somit kommt dem Sehsinn eine Art Vormachtstellung zu, die für den Erkenntnisgewinn in der westlichen Philosophiegeschichte eine entscheidende Rolle spielt. Verantwortlich hierfür ist die Verknüpfung des Sehens mit dem Verstehen bei gleichzeitiger oberster Priorisierung von rationaler Erkenntnis.[58] Die Priorisierung des Sehsinns wurde, wie Jütte es ausführlich darlegt, nie wirklich in Frage gestellt; sie prägt letztlich das westliche, logozentristische Denken und damit die gesamte westliche Kultur bis heute:[59] »Cogito ergo sum« basiert auf dem ›sehenden Verstand‹ und der Abspaltung dessen zu allem Leiblichen, an das ein Fühlen geknüpft wäre. Während dem Sehsinn Eigenschaften von Klarheit und Wahrheitsgewinn zugeordnet werden, fungiert der Tastsinn gewissermaßen als sein dunkler Gegenspieler: Dem Tasten und Fühlen wird gemeinhin eine niedere, bisweilen sogar schmutzige Funktion eingeräumt, die auf die stark sexuelle Konnotation dieses Sinns zurückzuführen ist.[60] Das Tasten wurde, wie es Harrasser aufzeigt, als »subjektiv, zu ungenau, zu gefährlich nah an der Lust« erachtet und an den Rand gedrängt.[61] Auf den Zusammenhang zwischen Berührung und Lust

---

55 Über die genaue Anzahl scheint unter Forscher*innen keine Einigkeit zu herrschen. Angaben schwanken zwischen 6 und 13 Sinnen, je nachdem, welche Sinne genau hinzugezählt werden (beispielsweise Selbstwahrnehmung/Propiozeption, Schmerzempfinden/Nozizeption und Hunger-Durst-Empfinden/viszeraler Sinn). Vgl. z.B. Stefan Dörner (2010): »Wie viele Sinne hat der Mensch?« Handelsblatt: https://www.handelsblatt.com/technik/forschung-innovation/schneller-schlau/schneller-schlau-wie-viele-sinne-hat-der-mensch/3646904.html (letzter Zugriff: 20.10.21).

56 Vgl. Robert Jütte (2000): »Die Geschichte der Sinne. Von der Antike bis zum Cyberspace.« München: C.H. Beck, S. 73.

57 Vgl. Jütte 2000, S. 73.

58 Vgl. Waltraud Naumann-Beyer (2003): *Anatomie der Sinne im Spiegel von Philosophie, Ästhetik, Literatur.* Köln: Böhlau Verlag, S. 204.

59 Vgl. Jütte 2000, S. 75.

60 Vgl. Jütte 2000, S. 113: »An der starken sexuellen Konnotation des Tastsinns bis weit in die Frühe Neuzeit hinein kann in der Tat kaum ein Zweifel bestehen.« Tatsächlich wird das Tastsinn in seiner reproduktiven Funktion von Aristoteles teilweise auch als »lebenserhaltend« hervorgehoben und also positiv gewertet – die Zuordnung von Tastsinn und Trieb bleibt damit aber aufrechterhalten. Vgl. Naumann-Beyer 2003, S. 206.

61 Katrin Harrasser (2017): »Einleitung.« In: dies. (Hg.): *Wissensgeschichte des Tastsinns:* Frankfurt am Main: Campus Verlag, S. 11. Vgl. auch Sandra Fluhrer und Alexander Waszynski (2020): »Einleitung.« In: dies. (Hg.): *Tangieren – Szenen des Berührens.* Baden-Baden: Rombach Wissenschaft, S. 7.

verweist auch Nancy: »The first and previously most widespread sense of *rühr* was that of sexual pleasure.«[62] Er schreibt außerdem: »We understand that the most widespread taboo relates to touch.«[63] Damit verortet sich der Tastsinn gesellschaftlich im Bereich des Vulgären, Unreinen, vom Begehren gesteuerten – potentiell sogar Verbotenen.[64] Die ›verruchte‹ Konnotation des Tastsinns ist sicherlich auch ein Grund dafür, dass dieser Sinn in der Wissenschaftsgeschichte verhältnismäßig wenig Aufmerksamkeit erfahren hat.[65]

Nachdem bereits aufgezeigt wurde, inwieweit die Priorisierung des Sehsinns abendländisches Denken und Kultur geprägt haben, erscheint es wenig verwunderlich, dass auch die westliche Theatertradition starke okularzentristische Tendenzen aufweist: Das Theater gilt als ein Ort des *Sehens*. Bereits die Etymologie des Begriffs ›Theater‹ verweist auf seinen engen Bezug zur Tätigkeit des Schauens bzw. Zu-Schauens.[66] Spätestens seit der Entstehung der barocken Guckkastenbühne funktioniert das Theater als ein *Schauraum*, in welchem das – durch das Portal wie ein Bild gerahmte – Bühnengeschehen aus der Distanz heraus betrachtet wird.[67] Somit ist die primäre Rezeptionstätigkeit im Theater (und damit auch die des Bühnentanzes) eine visuelle, die sich in die okularzentristisch-logozentristische Tradition eines ›Sehens um zu Verstehen‹ einfügt.

Nach dem kurzen Exkurs zum Okularzentrismus und seinen Implikationen für das Theater komme ich nun zurück zu den Berührungen, die im Rahmen des choreografischen Settings bei CO-TOUCH stattfinden. Weiter oben habe ich herausgestellt, dass das Berühren und Berührt-Werden hier die eigentliche Choreografie darstellen: In

---

[62]   Jean-Luc Nancy (2017): »Rühren, Berühren, Aufruhr.« In: ders./Van Reeth, Adèle (Hg.): *Coming.* New York: Fordham University Press, S. 111.

[63]   Nancy 2017, S. 112.

[64]   Vgl. Jütte 2000, S. 82. Auf die aktuelle Ausdehnung der Konnotation von Tasten/Berühren als etwas Verbotenem im Zuge der Corona-Pandemie werde ich weiter unten noch spezifisch eingehen.

[65]   Vgl. Jütte 2000, S. 22. Es muss an dieser Stelle angefügt werden, dass heute dem Tastsinn im Bereich Produktdesign neue Aufmerksamkeit zu Teil wird, etwa in der fortschreitenden Entwicklung von Touch-Screens. Eine Reflexion darüber, inwieweit dies jenseits von Zwecken der Konsumsteigerung auch eine Auswirkung auf die gesellschaftliche Rolle des Tastsinns haben mag, muss Aufgabe der Medienwissenschaften sein und kann an dieser Stelle nicht unternommen werden.

[66]   Der Begriff stammt aus dem griechischen ›theatron‹, welcher sich vom griechischen Verb ›theastai‹ für ›schauen‹, ›zuschauen‹, ›betrachten‹ ableitet. Vgl. Digitales Wörterbuch der deutschen Sprache. Eintrag ›Theater‹. https://www.dwds.de/wb/Theater (letzter Zugriff: 03.02.22).

[67]   Vgl. hierzu z.B. Erika Fischer-Lichte (1999): *Kurze Geschichte des deutschen Theaters.* Basel und Tübingen: Francke, S. 109. Natürlich spielt neben dem Sehen auch das Hören als ein weiterer sogenannter Fernsinn im Theater eine wichtige Rolle. Das Tasten als Nahsinn ist dahingegen aus dem Schauraum Theater ausgeschlossen.

deren Rezeption wird das Fühlen als solches durch einen gezielt inszenierten Entzug des Sehsinns zur Sensation – zur Sensation im ursprünglichen Sinne, empfindend.[68] Der Versuch, diese Aufführung rezeptions*ästhetisch* zu beschreiben, lässt daher einen Rückgriff auf die ursprüngliche Bedeutung von Ästhetik, die antike Aisthesis, als weiterführend erscheinen. Gleichzeitig untergräbt CO-TOUCH jedoch die in der Aisthesis traditionell angelegte okularzentristisch geprägte Sinneshierarchie: Vielmehr wird hier das Tasten und Fühlen sowohl zum Wahrnehmungsmodus als auch zum ästhetischen Material. Damit ist das In-Berührung-Sein gleichzeitig Mittel und ›Thema‹ der Arbeit. Es gibt hier keine Choreografie, deren Ästhetik sich nach visuellen Maßstäben beschreiben ließe. Das Ästhetische der Choreografie erschließt sich vielmehr ausschließlich mittels leiblich-taktiler Rezeption. Um dieser Feststellung gerecht zu werden, erscheint, wie oben vorgeschlagen, eine Ergänzung des Ästhetikbegriffes um den Begriff der Praxis als sehr fruchtbar.

Insbesondere drei Aspekte von Praxis erscheinen für die Rezeptionsbeschreibung einer taktilen partizipativen Choreografie anschlussfähig: Diese seien hier mit Prozesshaftigkeit, Leiblichkeit und Eigensinn bezeichnet und sollen im Folgenden kurz umrissen werden. Der Praxisbegriff richtet den Fokus auf das (menschliche) Tun in seiner Prozesshaftigkeit. Hetzel spricht in diesem Zusammenhang vom Vollzugscharakter der Praxis.[69] Mit Bezug auf Aristoteles formuliert er: »Als praxis gilt in der griechischen Alltagssprache ein umfassendes Wirksamkeits- und Vollzugsgefüge, das nicht auf intentionale und regelgeleitete menschliche Handlungen im engeren Sinne beschränkt bleibt.«[70] Vielmehr sei die Praxis selbstreferentiell, habe also ihr Ziel in sich selbst.[71] Vergleichbar beschreibt auch Bedorf Praxis als ein Geschehen, »dessen Sinn im Vollzug selbst besteht.«[72] Mit dem Fokus auf das Prozesshafte lässt sich mit dem Praxisbegriff im Beispiel CO-TOUCH die Tatsache hervorheben, dass es sich um eine Art Fühlen im Vollzug handelt. Die Rezeption als aktiver Zustand des In-Berührung-Seins scheint sich so angemessen fassen zu lassen. Ein zweiter, mit ihrer Prozesshaftigkeit verbundener Aspekt von Praxis ist die Tatsache, dass sich eine wie auch immer geartete Praxis erst durch ein Ausüben ihrer selbst begreifen und beschreiben lässt. Hetzel hält fest: »Was Praxis ist, lässt sich immer nur klären und erfahren, wenn wir uns in eine

---

68   Die Herkunft des Wortes stammt aus dem Französischen »sensation«, »die Empfindung« bzw. aus dem Lateinischen »sensatus«: »empfindend«. Vgl. Wolfgang Pfeifer et al. (1993): Etymologisches Wörterbuch des Deutschen. Eintrag ›Sensation‹. https://www.dwds.de/wb/etymwb/Sensation (letzter Zugriff: 20.09.21).

69   Vgl. Hetzel 2021, S. 82: »Praxis erweist sich damit als ein durativer oder performativer Begriff, als ein Begriff, der den Vollzug des Tätigseins betont.«

70   Hetzel 2021, S. 72.

71   Vgl. Hetzel 2021, S. 85.

72   Bedorf 2015, S. 129.

Praxis einüben. Praxis lässt sich insofern nicht soziologisch von außen beobachten.«[73] Damit stellt sich gleichzeitig ein unmittelbarer Bezug zwischen Praxis und Körper ein, denn ein Erfahren von Praxis über das Einüben bedeutet unausweichlich ein körperliches Einüben: So betont Bedorf, dass sich »zwar Praktiken ohne Dinge, nicht aber ohne Körper denken« lassen.[74] Diesen Aspekt machen auch Klein und Goebel stark:

> Handeln ist in praxistheoretischen Ansätzen als Ausschnitt einer Praktik definiert, die vom Körper getragen oder wahrgenommen wird. Praktiken vollziehen sich somit immer in materieller und körperlicher Ko-Aktivität mit anderen Subjekten, Dingen, Artefakten, den räumlich-materiellen sowie situationalen Rahmungen.[75]

Bedorf verweist allerdings auf die Problematik, dass der Körperbegriff in den Praxistheorien implizit einen cartesianischen Körper-Geist-Dualismus weitertragen, den sie eigentlich überwinden wollen. Er schlägt stattdessen vor, Praxis mit einem phänomenologischen Leibbegriff zu denken. Somit wäre das körperliche Einüben der Praxis immer auch ein leibliches Einüben. Ein drittes relevantes Charakteristikum des Praxisbegriffes ist seine Betonung auf Offenheit und Weiterentwicklung. Praxis als menschliches Tun im leiblichen Vollzug zu verstehen, beinhaltet immer auch die Möglichkeit, diesen Vollzug zu erweitern und damit seine impliziten Regeln ›eigensinnig‹ zu überschreiten.[76] Schmidt bezeichnet dies als die »inhärente Transformativität der Praxis, ihr Potential, mit jedem erneuten praktischen Vollzug Variationen hervorzubringen und somit in die Richtung abweichender, ebenso fragiler Ordnungsgefüge zu zeigen.«[77] Vergleichbar versteht auch Hetzel mit Aristoteles Praxis als

> denjenigen Bereich des Seins [...], in dem alles immer auch ›anders sein, werden oder sich verhalten kann‹. Ästhetische Praktiken wären dann als Weisen des Umgangs mit Offenheit und Kontingenz zu verstehen, die diese Kontingenz nicht einfach nur abarbeiten, sondern als Movens einer Bewegung nutzen, in deren Vollzug sich immer wieder neue Praxismöglichkeiten abzeichnen.[78]

Mit der Betonung des offenen Verlaufs von Praxis soll schließlich auf eine weitere Besonderheit bei der Rezeption von CO-TOUCH verwiesen werden, nämlich auf die Möglichkeit der aktiven Einflussnahme der Teilnehmenden auf das Geschehen.

---

73 Hetzel 2021, S. 89.
74 Bedorf 2015, S. 130.
75 Gabriele Klein und Hanna Katharina Göbel (2017): »Einleitung.« In: dies. (Hg.): *Performance und Praxis.* Bielefeld: transcript, S. 16.
76 Vgl. Schmidt 2021, S. 198.
77 Schmidt 2021, S. 198.
78 Hetzel 2021, S. 90.

Die Ausführungen zu den Begriffen Aisthetik und Praxis führen mich schließlich zum Begriffspaar ästhetische Praxis. Hetzel schlägt hierfür folgende Definition vor: »Als ästhetische Praxis verstehe ich im Anschluss an Aristoteles einen selbstzweckhaften und zugleich ›leiblichen, vollsinnlich eingebundenen‹ Vollzug, der sich nicht handlungstheoretisch beschreiben lässt.«[79] Ausgehend von dieser Definition lässt sich das Berühren und Berührtwerden bei CO-TOUCH als eine Tätigkeit fassen, die sich über ihren aktiven und leiblichen Vollzug definiert, während dieser Vollzug in seiner spezifischen choreografischen Rahmung gleichzeitig als ein ästhetischer zu bezeichnen ist.[80] Die leiblich-taktile Partizipation bei CO-TOUCH lässt sich damit nicht nur als spezifischer Rezeptionsmodus, sondern gleichzeitig auch als ästhetische Praxis verstehen. Dies bedeutet auch, die bedeutende Rolle anzuerkennen, die hier den partizipierenden Rezipient*innen zuteil wird: Vielleicht beginnt jemand so wild zu tanzen, dass die Situation außer Kontrolle gerät, vielleicht verweigert sich jemand der Berührung, vielleicht ist sich jemand zu unsicher, um überhaupt je vom Stuhl aufzustehen, vielleicht bringt die Berührung jemanden zum Weinen – unzählige Möglichkeiten potentieller Abweichungen sind denkbar. Während der Ablauf der Aufführung durch choreografische und akustische Setzungen strukturiert und durch das fürsorgliche Begleiten der Performer*innen durchaus gelenkt wird, ist der Verlauf der Choreografie, dort, wo sie sich auf die teilnehmenden Körper ausdehnt, offen. Mit dem Begriff der ästhetischen Praxis steht damit nicht die Frage nach CO-TOUCH als einem choreografischen Werk im Vordergrund, sondern es wird der Prozess des gemeinsamen Praktizierens im Rahmen der korporal-sensuell partizipativen Choreografie betont.

Sicherlich lassen sich, dies sei eingewendet, auch traditionelle, primär visuelle Formen der Kunst- oder Theaterrezeption als ästhetische Praxis im Sinne eines sinnlichen Vollzuges verstehen: Auch das Sehen (und Hören) sind an eine leibliche Wahrnehmung geknüpft. Ich habe aber ausgeführt, dass das Zuschauen im Theater von einer okularzentristisch-logozentristischen Tradition (»Sehen um zu Verstehen«) geprägt ist, die wiederum auf einem hierarchisch angelegten Körper-Geist-Dualismus basiert. Meine Ausführungen zur Rezeption taktiler Choreografie als ästhetische Praxis legen hingegen nahe, dass hier die leiblich-taktile Wahrnehmung im Vordergrund steht: Es entfaltet sich dabei eine taktile Ästhetik,[81] welche ein Gegenmodell zur okularzentristischen Sinneshierarchie darstellt. In der exemplarisch vorgestellten Arbeit

---

[79] Hetzel 2021, S. 89. Zum Begriffspaar ›ästhetische Praxis‹ vergleiche auch Rolf Elberfeld und Stefan Krankenhagen (2017): »Einleitung – Ästhetische Praxis als Gegenstand und Methode kulturwissenschaftlicher Forschung.« In: dies. (Hg.): *Ästhetische Praxis als Gegenstand und Methode kulturwissenschaftlicher Forschung*. Paderborn: Wilhelm Fink, S. 17.

[80] Vgl. hierzu Fußnote 50.

[81] Sie tritt, mit Seel, »in Erscheinung« und tut streng genommen genau das zugleich nicht, da es sich um eine Ästhetik handelt, die mit Licht-Metaphern nicht zu fassen ist. Vgl. Martin Seel (2000): *Ästhetik des Erscheinens*. München: Carl Hanser.

CO-TOUCH wird das Konzept des Theaters als Schauraum so unterlaufen. An seiner Stelle entsteht hier ein performativer *Fühlraum.* Die Fokussierung auf den Tastsinn qua gezielt inszeniertem ›Blind-Stellen‹ der Teilnehmerinnen lässt sich somit auch als eine Kritik an einem leib-feindlichen, gar bigotten Wertesystem westlicher Philosophie verstehen. Das Praktizieren eines berührenden In-Kontakt-Tretens ist hier nicht vulgär oder ›schmutzig‹, sondern ästhetische Quintessenz. Hierin liegt meines Erachtens die politische Potentialität einer solchen taktilen Choreografie begründet.

4. Berühren – eine ästhetische Praxis ohne aktuelle Praxis?

In Anbetracht der grassierenden Covid-19-Pandemie tritt uns die politische Dimension von Berührung nun plötzlich an unerwarteten Stellen und mit ungeahnter Wucht entgegen. Nachdem ich das in einem partizipativen choreografischen Rahmen statt-findende Berühren als ästhetische Praxis beschrieben habe, will ich daher zuletzt den Fokus auf den aktuellen zeitlichen Kontext lenken, während dem der vorliegende Artikel entstanden ist. Seit dem Ausbruch der Corona-Pandemie im März 2020 hat sich unser Blick auf Berührung drastisch verschoben. Eine Fremde an der Hand zu berühren, so wie im Beispiel CO-TOUCH beschrieben, stellte zum Zeitpunkt der Aufführung im Januar 2020 eine alltägliche Geste dar, die innerhalb des beschriebenen performativ-choreografischen Kontextes ästhetisch bedeutsam wurde. Doch dieselbe Geste ist in-zwischen alles andere als alltäglich, vielmehr ist sie mit Gefahr konnotiert; eine Geste, die in der Öffentlichkeit kaum noch gesehen, empfangen wird – schon gar nicht unter Fremden! Im folgenden letzten Abschnitt des Beitrags soll ein kurzer Blick auf den aktuellen gesellschaftlichen Status von Berührung geworfen werden, um schließlich zu fragen: Wie wirkt sich die gesellschaftliche ›Berührungsabstinenz‹ auf ein Nachden-ken über Berührung als ästhetische Praxis aus?

Seit März 2020 erlebt die gültige gesellschaftliche Berührungsordnung und die damit verbundene Konnotation von Berührung einen dramatischen Wandel: Ehemals takt-volle Verhaltensweisen wie Händeschütteln oder freundschaftliches Umarmen sind suspendiert, gewissermaßen ›über Nacht‹ in eine Gefahrenzone gerückt worden:[82] »Durch die Corona-Pandemie verschiebt sich allgemein das Verhältnis von öffentli-chem Raum und familiärem Nahraum. Wir werden daran gewöhnt, dass alle, die nicht zur familiären Nahgruppe gehören, potentiell bedrohlich sind.«[83] Damit werden Gesten

---

82   Vgl. hierzu Gesa Lindemann (2020): *Die Ordnung der Berührung. Staat, Gewalt und Kritik in Zeiten der Coronakrise*, Weilerswist: Velbrück Wissenschaft, S. 12/13. Kritisch muss hierzu al-lerdings angemerkt werden, dass Lindemann von »familiärem Nahraum« spricht und damit nicht-familiäre Formen des Zusammenlebens ausschließt.
83   Lindemann 2020, S. 58.

der Nähe, Zärtlichkeit oder freundschaftlicher körperlicher Kontaktaufnahme zu gefährlichem, sogar illegalem Verhalten.[84] Daraus ergibt sich zwangsläufig, dass Theater- und Tanzperformances, bei denen das Berühren gleichsam Form und Inhalt ist, zwischenzeitlich von der Bildfläche – oder besser gesagt: aus der Fühlzone – verschwunden sind: Wir (als Mitglieder der Gesellschaft) sollen überall außerhalb unseres eigenen Haushaltes voneinander Abstand halten.[85] Der Staat greift dabei soweit in die Berührungsordnung der Gesellschaft ein, dass auch ein temporäres Aussetzen dieser Berührungsordnung mit künstlerischen Mitteln nicht mehr möglich (und epidemiologisch auch nicht sinnvoll) ist. Wenn schon der Aufenthalt in einer ›normalen‹ Theatersituation zum Ansteckungsrisiko wird, so erscheinen partizipative Aufführungsformate, die über Berührung funktionieren, aus aktueller Perspektive geradezu undenkbar. Während sich in der Theaterlandschaft in den vergangenen eineinhalb Jahren ein bisher so nicht dagewesener Digitalisierungsschub konstatieren lässt, so sind Formate, in denen es um eine taktile Partizipation geht, im Zuge dieser Digitalisierung buchstäblich von der Bildfläche verschwunden: Denn das leibliche Berühren und Berührtwerden lässt sich eben auf diese Bildfläche nicht übertragen. Auch im Hinblick auf Öffnungen der Theaterhäuser mit 2- oder 3-G-Regelung erscheint es fragwürdig, wann – oder ob überhaupt – künstlerische Formate, die mittels Taktilität (enges körperliches Beisammensein einschließlich gegenseitigen Anfassens!) funktionieren, wieder stattfinden werden. Es wurde festgestellt, dass die hier besprochene partizipative Performance einen künstlerischen Rahmen bietet, in dem Teilnehmende Berührung als ästhetische Praxis erleben bzw. vollziehen können. Das Angebot taktiler Choreografien wie der hier vorgestellten, qua Berührungen zwischen Teilnehmenden und Performer*innen einen anti-okularzentristischen Reflexionsrahmen für Berührung zu schaffen, entfällt damit pikanterweise just in dem Moment, in dem es gesellschaftlich besonders aktuell – und damit wahrscheinlich auch notwendig – wäre.

Die aktuellen Entwicklungen scheinen sich nun wie eine zusätzliche Folie über die hier vorgestellten Erkenntnisse zu legen, hinter der diese merkwürdig zu oszillieren beginnen: Einerseits kommt es zu einer möglichen Verzerrung der Wahrnehmung und Beurteilung der hier beispielhaft angeführten Berührungsszene: Löst ihre Lektüre aufgrund der beschriebenen körperlichen Nähe Befremden, Angst, gar Ekel aus? In diese Richtung jedenfalls spekuliert Lindemann, wenn sie schreibt: »Es dürfte interessant sein, ob bzw. wie sich unter solchen Bedingungen neue Ekel- und Scham-

---

84 Interessanterweise mutet den neuen freundschaftlichen ›Ersatzberührungen‹ wie etwa Ellbogen- oder Fußeinschlag etwas Grobes an, während zärtliche Gesten wie der Wangenkuss – zumindest zum Zeitpunkt des Verfassens dieses Beitrags – tatsächlich aus der Öffentlichkeit verschwunden sind.

85 Vgl. Lindemann 2020, S. 58.

schwellen entwickeln.«[86] Andererseits stellt sich beim Thematisieren von Berührung als ästhetischer Praxis fast zwangsläufig auch eine gewisse Melancholie ein, weil ihre Bedeutung in Anbetracht einer fortdauernden Berührungs-Abwesenheit umso plastischer hervorzutreten scheint. Womöglich weckt das Lesen der angeführten Beispiele eben nicht nur Befremden, sondern auch Sehnsucht. Wie sich der gesellschaftliche Umgang mit Berührung in Anbetracht aggressiver Pandemien entwickeln und verändern wird, darüber könnte an dieser Stelle allenfalls spekuliert werden. Pessimistische Stimmen prognostizieren eine nachhaltige Veränderung der gängigen Berührungsordnung.[87] Womöglich werden sich aber auch neue Wege finden, Berührung außerhalb von Wohn- oder Lebensgemeinschaften und also auch in choreografisch-performativen Kontexten wieder möglich zu machen. Berührung stellt schlussendlich einen so wesentlichen Pfeiler menschlichen (ja überhaupt allen) Lebens dar, dass es fragwürdig erscheint, ob sie sich dauerhaft vermeiden und verbieten lässt. Wie Kearney schreibt: »Because without touch there is no life.«[88]

5. Fazit

Der Beitrag stellte die Frage nach den Möglichkeiten einer rezeptionsästhetischen Beschreibung von choreografischen oder performativen Formaten, die über eine taktile Involvierung des teilnehmenden Publikums funktionieren. Zur Beantwortung dieser Frage wurde zunächst aufgeführt, wie sich die hier stattfindende korporal-sensuelle bzw. leiblich-taktile Partizipation als spezifische Form von Rezeption verstehen lässt. In einem zweiten Schritt wurde dann anhand des Beispiels CO-TOUCH vorgeschlagen, die hier stattfindende Berührungsrezeption als ästhetische Praxis zu begreifen. Die Verwendung dieses Begriffspaars hebt die Bedeutung der leiblichen und präsentischen Dimension des performativen Geschehens hervor. Außerdem wird mit dem Verständnis der Rezeption von taktilen Choreografien als ästhetischer Praxis der individuelle Handlungsspielraum jedes*r partizipierend Rezipierenden und die damit verbundene Offenheit des Verlaufs betont. Berührung im Rahmen partizipativer künstlerischer Formate als ästhetische Praxis erfahrbar zu machen bedeutet, einen Raum zu schaffen, in dem die Wahrnehmung für Berührung geschärft und die Bedeutung von Berührung reflektiert werden kann – einen Raum, in dem, so lässt sich

---

86   Lindemann 2020, S. 59.
87   So sagt Lindemann beispielsweise tatsächlich einen Niedergang der Paartänze voraus. Vgl. Lindemann 2020, S. 59.
88   Richard Kearney (2015): What is Carnal Hermeneutics? In: *New Literary History*, 2015, Vol. 46, S. 103.

nach den hier angestellten Überlegungen folgern, Berühren und Berührt-Werden *ästhetisch* erfahrbar werden.

Diese Erfahrung lässt sich nur vermitteln, wenn Berührung gleichzeitig künstlerisches Mittel und Zweck ist: Eine taktile Choreografie kann ästhetisches Potential nur qua Taktilität entfalten. Dieses Spezifikum wurde zuletzt im Hinblick auf die aktuelle, durch die Corona-Pandemie geprägte gesellschaftliche Situation reflektiert. Die notgedrungenen Versuche vieler Spielstätten, mit ›digitalen Bühnen‹ und Livestreams auf die Pandemie-Situation zu reagieren, bedeuten für Formate, die über leiblich-taktile Rezeption funktionieren, einen Rückschlag. Gleichzeitig stellen aber gerade diese Formate, wie am Beispiel CO-TOUCH aufgezeigt, eine Möglichkeit dar, Berühren und Berührt-Werden als ästhetische Praxis jenseits der okularzentristischen Ästhetik-Tradition zu vollziehen. Diese Praxis entfällt bezeichnenderweise genau in dem Moment, in dem die Verordnung einer ›Berührungsabstinenz‹ in Kraft getreten ist und in dem eine künstlerische Reflexion darüber sicherlich besonders von Bedeutung wäre. Mit Spannung bleibt zu beobachten, wie Praktiken des Berührens wieder aufgenommen, wie sie sich verändern oder weiter entwickeln werden – in künstlerischen Formaten und darüber hinaus.

Literaturliste

Aristoteles (2020): *Über die Seele*. Übersetzt und herausgegeben von Gernot Krapinger. Stuttgart: Reclam.

Bedorf, Thomas (2015): »Leibliche Praxis. Zum Körperbegriff in den Praxistheorien.« In: Alkemeyer, Thomas/Schürmann, Volker/Volbers, Jörg (Hg.): *Praxis denken. Konzepte und Kritik*. Wiesbaden: Springer VS, S. 129-150.

Bishop, Claire (2012): *Artificial Hells. Participatory Art and the Politics of Spectatorship*. London/New York: Verso.

Bishop, Claire (2006): *Participation. Documents of Contemporary Art*. London: MIT Press.

Bourriaud, Nicolas (Hg.) (2002): *Postproduction. Culture as Screenplay: How Art Reprograms the World*. New York: Sternberg Press.

Bourriaud, Nicolas (2010): *Relational Aesthetics*. Monts: Les presses du réel.

Brandstetter, Gabriele (2013): »Listening«. Kinesthetic Awareness in Contemporary Dance, in: dies./Egert, Gerko/Zubarik, Sabine (Hg.): *Touching and Being Touched. Kinesthesia and Empathy in Dance and Movement*. Berlin/Boston: De Gruyter, S. 163-179.

Czirak, Adam (2012): *Partizipation der Blicke. Szenerien des Sehens und Gesehenwerdens in Theater und Performance*. Bielefeld: transcript.

Dörner, Stephan (2010): »Wie viele Sinne hat der Mensch?« Handelsblatt: https://www.handelsblatt.com/technik/forschung-innovation/schneller-schlau/schneller-schlau-wie-viele-sinne-hat-der-mensch/3646904.html (letzter Zugriff: 20.09.21).

Elberfeld, Rolf/Krankenhagen, Stefan (2017): »Einleitung – Ästhetische Praxis als Gegenstand und Methode kulturwissenschaftlicher Forschung.« In: dies. (Hg.): *Ästhetische Praxis als*

Gegenstand und Methode kulturwissenschaftlicher Forschung. Paderborn: Wilhelm Fink, S. 7-25.

Feldhoff, Silke (2009): »Zwischen Spiel und Politik: Partizipation als Strategie und Praxis in der bildenden Kunst.« https://opus4.kobv.de/opus4-udk/frontdoor/deliver/index/docId/26/file/Feldhoff_Silke.pdf (letzter Zugriff: 20.09.21).

Fischer-Lichte, Erika (1999): *Kurze Geschichte des deutschen Theaters.* Tübingen und Basel: Francke.

Fluhrer, Sandra/Waszynski, Alexander (2020): »Einleitung.« In: dies. (Hg.): *Tangieren – Szenen des Berührens.* Baden-Baden: Rombach Wissenschaft, S. 7-17.

Harrasser, Katrin (2017): »Einleitung.« In: dies. (Hg.): *Wissensgeschichte des Tastsinns.* Frankfurt am Main: Campus Verlag, S. 7-14.

Hetzel, Andreas (2021): »Im Vollzug. Praxis als Grundbegriff einer Aristotelischen Ästhetik.« In: Corsten, Michael (Hg.): *Praxis Ausüben Begreifen.* Weilerswist: Velbrück Wissenschaft, S. 69-94.

Jütte, Robert (2000): *Die Geschichte der Sinne. Von der Antike bis zum Cyberspace.* München: C.H. Beck.

Kearney, Richard (2015): »What is Carnal Hermeneutics?« In: *New Literary History*, 2015, Vol. 46, S. 99-124.

Keller, Julia (2021): »From Studio to Dining Table: Rirkrit Tiravanija.« Schirn: https://www.schirn.de/en/magazine/whats_cooking/vom_atelier_an_den_esstisch_rirkrit_tiravanija/ (letzter Zugriff: 11.10.21).

Kemp, Wolfgang (2015): *Der explizite Betrachter.* Konstanz: Konstanz University Press.

Klein, Gabriele/Göbel, Hanna Katharina (2017): »Einleitung.« In: dies. (Hg.): *Performance und Praxis. Praxeologische Erkundungen in Tanz, Theater, Sport und Alltag.* Bielefeld: transcript, S. 7-42.

Kravagna, Christian (1999): »Arbeit an der Gemeinschaft. Modelle partizipatorischer Praxis.« Transversal: https://transversal.at/transversal/1204/kravagna/de (letzter Zugriff: 21.09.21).

Lindemann, Gesa (2020): *Die Ordnung der Berührung. Staat, Gewalt und Kritik in Zeiten der Coronakrise.* Weilerswist: Velbrück Wissenschaft.

Nancy, Jean-Luc (2017): »Rühren, Berühren, Aufruhr.« In: ders./Van Reeth, Adèle (Hg.): *Coming.* New York: Fordham University Press, S. 101-115.

Naumann-Beyer, Waltraud (2003): *Anatomie der Sinne im Spiegel von Philosophie, Ästhetik, Literatur.* Köln: Böhlau Verlag.

Pfeifer, Wolfgang et al. (1993): *Etymologisches Wörterbuch des Deutschen.* Eintrag ›Sensation‹. https://www.dwds.de/wb/etymwb/Sensation (letzter Zugriff: 20.09.21).

Pfeifer, Wolfgang et al. (1993): *Etymologisches Wörterbuch des Deutschen.* Eintrag ›partizipieren‹. https://www.dwds.de/wb/etymwb/partizipieren (letzter Zugriff: 20.09.21).

Rancière, Jacques (2009): *Der emanzipierte Zuschauer.* Wien: Passagen Verlag.

Roselt, Jens (2012): »Den Augen trauen: Theater und Phänomenologie.« In: Fischer-Lichter, Erika/Czirak, Adam/Jost, Torsten et al. (Hg.): *Die Aufführung. Diskurs – Macht – Analyse.* München: Wilhelm Fink, S. 263-273.

Scheurle, Christoph (2017): »Kunst als politische Partizipation – politische Partizipation als Kunst?« Kulturelle Bildung Online: https://www.kubi-online.de/artikel/kunst-politische-partizipation-politische-partizipation-kunst (letzter Zugriff: 20.09.21).

Schmidt, Jens (2021): »Ästhetische Praxis als ökologische Konzeption. Situationen relational-divergierender Rezeptionspraxis.« In: Corsten, Michael (Hg.): *Praxis. Ausüben. Begreifen.* Weilerswist: Velbrück Verlag, S. 197-219.

Schweppenhäuser, Gerhard (2007): *Ästhetik. Philosophische Grundlagen und Schlüsselbegriffe.* Frankfurt am Main: Campus.

Seel, Martin (2000): *Ästhetik des Erscheinens.* München: Carl Hanser.

Seitz, Hanne (2012): »Impulsvortrag Partizipation. Formen der Beteiligung im zeitgenössischen Theater.« http://www.was-geht-berlin.de/sites/default/files/hanne_seitz_partizipation_ 2012.pdf (letzter Zugriff: 13.05.20).

Siegmund, Gerald (2016): »Das Problem der Partizipation.« Goethe Institut: https://www. goethe.de/ins/es/de/kul/sup/bew/20708712.html (letzter Zugriff: 21.09.21).

Spohn, Anna (2016): »Die Idee der Partizipation und der Begriff der Praxis.« In: Kauppert, Michael/Eberl, Heidrun (Hg.): *Ästhetische Praxis.* Berlin: Springer VS, S. 37-54.

Ternes, Bernd (2000): »Zum Begriff der Wahrnehmung/Aisthesis.« Aisthesis Verlag: https:// www.aisthesis.de/epages/63645342.sf/de_DE/?ObjectPath=/Shops/63645342/Categories/ AboutUs/Aisthesis/Begriff_Aisthesis (letzter Zugriff: 11.10.21).

Van Eikels, Kai (2019): »Vorlesungsskript ›Partizipation. Ansprüche und Wirklichkeiten des Politischen in den Künsten‹.« Die Kunst des Kollektiven: https://kunstdeskollektiven.wor dpress.com/2019/02/08/vorlesungsmanuskript-partizipation-ansprueche-und-wirklich keiten-des-politischen-in-den-kuensten/ (letzter Zugriff: 11.10.21).

Website Ballhaus Ost, Berlin. Information zur Produktion ›Hotel Berlin‹. https://www.ball hausost.de/produktionen/hotel-berlin/ (letzter Zugriff: 11.10.21).

Website Digitales Wörterbuch der deutschen Sprache. https://www.dwds.de (letzter Zugriff: 03.02.22)

Website Europäisches Zentrum der Künste, Hellerau. Information zur Produktion ›CO-TOUCH‹. https://www.hellerau.org/de/event/co-touch/ (letzter Zugriff: 21.09.21).

Antje Kley

Vulnerability and Masculinist Notions of Control in Late Capitalist Societies

Reading Paul Kalanithi's Autopathography *When Breath Becomes Air* (2016)

ABSTRACT: This article lays out how Kalanithi's international bestseller and Pulitzer Prize finalist uses the infrastructures of literature to negotiate the infrastructures and the masculinist values of the medical system. The text chronicles how a promising young male neurosurgeon becomes a terminal patient himself. This radical change of perspective is represented in ambivalent terms of embodiment, vulnerability, and relational being, and as a fall from the masculinist grace of medical discursive power. The text presents the medical hospital as a social space that, in its high-tech efficiency, is ill-equipped for the negotiation of the personally and culturally contradictory process of dying that, in late capitalist societies since the 1980s, predominantly takes place in its confines. With its literary means, the text explores a critical perspective on late capitalist societies' high-tech medical system that is geared towards the control of disease and cost at the expense of a supportive view of life's end. With its literary address of a neurosurgeon's experience of dying, *When Breath Becomes Air* offers an alternative form of knowledge production to currently dominant medical, care, insurance and legal discourses on death, and it advocates an ease of narrowly masculinist notions of control as key to more resonant social relations.

KEYWORDS: literature; medical system; vulnerability; illness; death; masculinity; relationality; resonance

1. Notions of vulnerability: an introduction

This article seeks to shed light on how Kalanithi's autobiographical text, prompted by the author's experience of fatal illness, uses the infrastructures of literature to negotiate the infrastructures and the masculinist values of the medical system.[1] My reading of the text is part of a larger project, entitled »Death Becomes Us«, concerned with US-American stories of the end of life since the 1980s.[2] The project is concerned with how

---

1   I want to thank my anonymous reviewers for their careful readings, helping me to clarify and strengthen the article's argument. Any remaining weaknesses are of course my own.
2   I am grateful to the *Knowledge Infrastructures Research Network* of the Regensburg *Center for International and Transnational Area Studies* (CITAS) as a stimulating context for this work and to

fictional and autobiographical writing socially embeds the experiences of dying and of losing a loved one. It argues that literary forms of knowledge production around mortality and death meet an acute social need in highly competitive capitalist performance societies: they connect professionally separate discourses of the body and the mind and develop a vocabulary to negotiate human vulnerability and mortality.[3] My study draws on and seeks to contribute to the fields of the medical humanities, narrative medicine, age and disability studies as well as cultural thanatology.[4]

With such diverse critics as Judith Butler and Ralf Schnell, I take the concept of vulnerability to denote the constitutive character of socially bound, embodied beings. In the more narrow but culturally dominant sense, »vulnerability« designates undesirable physical, mental or psychic limitations. Vulnerability in the wider and more all-encompassing sense precedes the distinction between healthy and ill bodies (Schnell 17-21, Butler 2020). »Vulnerability is not just the condition of being potentially harmed by another«, as Butler explains. »It names the porous and interdependent character of our bodily and social lives« (2020: 1). Assuming vulnerability as anthropologically given reminds us of the interdependence of living beings. The psychologist Kenneth Gergen speaks of »relational being« and recent work in palliative care and medical ethics has developed notions of »relational autonomy« (Gómez-Vírseda, Welsh/Ostgathe/Frewer/Bielefeldt) to redescribe acts and initiatives that we tend to ascribe to solipsistic individuals instead as socially embedded results of co-action, co-creation and dialogical developments in decision-making. Butler, Gambetti and Sabsay clarify that vulnerability does not imply passivity or social withdrawal: vulnerability is not »the opposite of resistance« and may be conceived as part of resistant practices (2016: 1-11, here 1).

---

the *Fritz-Thyssen-Stiftung* for its funding of a 6 months *LeseZeit* stipend in the summer 2020. The title »Death Becomes Us« is used by a growing number of articles and cultural productions concerned with a close examination of dying. Two examples are the journalist Pamela Skjolsvik's exploration of jobs related to death and the Presbyterian Minister Douglas E. Baker's review of McCullough's 2018 book *Remember Death: The Surprising Path to Living Hope.*

3 The cultural historian Anne Harrington bespeaks the need for connecting separate discourses of body and mind, science and experience in her well and widely received study *The Cure Within: A History of Mind-Body Medicine* (New York: Norton, 2008) 243-255. Literature is a discourse well-equipped to contribute to building such connections. The German literary critic Jürgen Link has described literature as an interdiscourse. Interdiscourses build bridges across compartmentalized bodies of knowledge and subjectivities. In this view, literary writing is engaged in remaking as it reports; it selects, accentuates, combines, and inflects partial bodies of knowledge from particular, historically changing discourses and areas of expertise – as, e.g., the medical system –, and it renders them relevant within particular cultural frames of reference. Readers may use these interdiscursively fictionalized worlds as models from which to extrapolate generatively intelligent clarification of the discursive interdependencies in their own past and present. See Kley 2016.

4 For work not mentioned elsewhere in this article, which historically and theoretically frames my concerns see Banerjee, Charon, Gilbert, and Kunow.

According to them, vulnerability implies the need for »collective forms of resistance and social transformation« rather than »the need for protection and the strengthening of paternalistic forms of power« (Butler, Gambetti, Sabsay 2016: 1). In this wide sense, the concept of ›vulnerability‹ implies reachability and relationality, a willingness to acknowledge and listen to others, an epistemic potential and attitude as well as a critique of sovereign power and control. *When Breath Becomes Air* undertakes a revaluation of human vulnerability in this relational sense. The text connects this revaluation with a critique of masculinist notions of control, which tend to cast vulnerability, embodiment and mortality in a decidedly negative light, presenting them as weaknesses to be fought.[5]

2. Illness as ›an agent of change‹

In his 1988 study *Disease and Representation: Images of Illness from Madness to AIDS*, Sander Gilman explains that, across time and cultures, imaginative representations of illness function as an antidote to the audience's fear of their own physical demise. According to Gilman, the audience's fear of a loss of control is kept in check as the representation bans it within its confines. Consuming the representation allows the recipient to develop a fantasy of wholeness and control that soothes his or her deeply rooted experience of exposure, instability, and vulnerability with the assertion that they are not affected by the harm depicted.

To some degree, Kalanithi's text participates in this pattern of containment, but it also significantly shakes it up, giving rise to an understanding of illness as »an agent of change«.[6] It does so by presenting a paradoxically positioned narrator-protagonist who is both a successful neurosurgeon and a terminally ill patient, telling his own story of illness as both a fall from the grace of medical credentialing and as a ›re-enchantment‹ of his own life and the lives of those close to him in and outside of the hospital. *When Breath Becomes Air* thus interweaves and overwrites a narrative pattern of restitution – »Yesterday I was healthy, today I am sick, but tomorrow I'll be healthy again« (Frank

---

5   In his 1991 essay »Autopathography: Women, Illness, and Lifewriting«, Thomas Couser emphasizes the gender codification of illness and its suppression inscribed in Western discourse: »the suppression of illness in literature has its subtext in the domination of discourse by masculinist assumptions […] the Western privileging of mind over body, the tendency to deny the body's intervention in intellectual and spiritual life« (68). This is not – at least not primarily – an argument about men and women. It is an argument about masculine and feminine codifications of certain qualities of habitualized thought and action.

6   This phrase comes from Eve Ensler's 2013 autopathography *In the Body of the World,* where the narrator speaks of cancer not as an enemy, but as »an alchemist, an agent of change« (8).

2013: 77) – with a pattern of undergoing a fundamental change of seeing and *being in the world.*

As a consumable popular book, *When Breath Becomes Air* does offer closure – provided by the author's wife who wrote the epilogue after her husband's death – and, with it, at least some measure of the reassurance to the reader that Gilman speaks about. But it also has a far more interesting, even if disturbing dimension. More than generically soothing a sense of vulnerability on the part of the reader, who may distance himself from the fate represented, the text prompts readers to join the dying narrator-protagonist, who cannot finish writing his account himself, in *reassessing the status of vulnerability* in a more general sense. The main indication for this other dimension of the text is its refraining from talking about disease in terms of an enemy to be defeated. *When Breath Becomes Air* questions this culturally pervasive rhetoric, which may frequently be found in patients' accounts of their encounters with life-threatening illness as well as in presentations of, e.g., cancer research.[7] The narrator recalls the bellicose but brittle reaction to bad medical news – »[w]e're gonna fight and beat this thing« – as an unrealistically optimistic form of crisis-denial and a knee-jerk »alternative to crushing despair« (96). The social theorist Laurent Berlant speaks of such optimism as »cruel.« »Cruel optimism« substitutes for a reckoning with one's own situation, »the built and affective infrastructure of the ordinary« (49). It indicates a »survival scenario« which, because of its cover-up nature, is in itself problematic: it keeps the threatened subject from »assess[ing] what's unraveling there« – here in the absorption of a fatal diagnosis – and thus from actually »measuring the impasse of living in the overwhelmingly present moment« (49).

In step with Berlant, Kalanithi's text exposes the rhetoric of ›fighting disease as an enemy‹ as a fundamentally helpless gesture. The narrator-protagonist himself accepts his fatal diagnosis with considerable ambiguity. On the one hand, as soon as he possibly can, he seeks to assert the masculinist sense of control that his profession bestows upon him. Insofar, he follows his father's insistence not to capitulate, an insistence in line

---

7   On the basis of the expansive readings he conducted for his 1997 study *Recovering Bodies*, Thomas Couser explains that the narrative pattern of the patient success story and its demand for a positive ending dominates the literary market. He speaks of »the tyranny of the comic plot« (Couser 2016: 4), which marginalizes narratives that do not tell a successful overcoming of illness and the restitution of a previous state of health. The medial sociologist Arthur W. Frank categorizes illness narratives into three corresponding patterns: »restitution« (Frank 2013: 75-96), »chaos,« (97-114), and »quest« (115-136). Frank explains that the »restitution narrative« may shade into the »quest narrative« when the confrontation with contingency is presented as a test to be mastered. »The risk of quest stories is like the risk of the Phoenix metaphor: they can present the burning process as too clean and the transformation as too complete, and they can implicitly deprecate those who fail to rise out of their own ashes« (Frank 2013: 135). Frank's view is explicitly reiterated in Anne Boyer's 2019 autobiography *The Undying.*

with the narrative of restitution the protagonist had been explicitly puzzled by time and again (127). Picking up on the ›cruelly optimistic‹ rhetoric of fighting disease, his father had stated that his son »was going to beat this thing, [he] would somehow be cured« (127). However, the doctor as patient, or the patient as doctor, feels forced to at least begin to look at his own life and his professional ambitions in ways *not* shaped by the logics of competition. He begins to relocate himself socially and affectively, in particular in relation to his family, shifting the scope of stories and encounters he invests his energies in. He thus defers the narrative of »restitution« with its rhetoric of masculinist self-assertion and success in the face of testing times. Knowing that he cannot win, he defers the ultimately cruel narrative of the »quest« for renewal, together with its tendency to romanticize or placate. Instead, the narrator-protagonist exposes himself *to* and engages *with* the experience of contingency and of *not* knowing »what life is in death,« as the epigraph by the Elizabethan poet and statesman Fulke Greville has it (ix). Kalanithi exposes himself to his own mortal being and channels his controlling energies, again with Fulke Greville, into an address of his audience: »Reader! Then make time, while you be,/ But steps to your eternity« (ix). There will be occasion to come back to the issue of time at the end of section 3. My point here is, though, that, with the decisive shift in perspective of its narrator-protagonist, the text blurs rather than reinforces the distinction between health, masculinist strength and control on the one hand and illness, weakness, emasculation and loss of control on the other. His narrative advocates a profoundly relaxed relation to time at the end of life.

Pacing the narrative pattern of restitution, the text engages a narrative pattern which closely examines desperation, the notion of the normal, radical change, as well as the protagonist's own bodily being and his relation to other people. The text still participates in, but also questions and begins to shed, the culturally dominant narrative pattern of restitution. This narrative pattern of battle, which is coded masculine in Western discourse, conceptualizes the body in technical terms as a mechanical entity that might have to be (and can be) repaired. This pattern casts illness as a bodily interruption of an entrepreneurial self that will rise like Phoenix from the ashes;[8] and the patient remains a monad or an autonomous entity complete in itself. Shedding a critical light on this rhetoric, while still being drawn to it at times, *When Breath Becomes Air* articulates a visceral witness account and a reevaluation of the *physical experience* as well as the *epistemology* of vulnerability, which are conventionally coded feminine and frequently marginalized in Western discourse in general and in the physicalist medical system in particular. As a patient the protagonist finally begins to understand the degree to which he – as much as others – has never been an autonomous entity complete in himself. As much as others, he is a manifestation of »relational existence«:

---

8   On the political sociology of the entrepreneurial self, see Broeckling.

his autonomy emerges from relations, community and co-ordinated action (Gergen 396-403).

3. Deflating masculinist notions of control in *When Breath Becomes Air*

The neurosurgeon and author Paul Kalanithi dies of lung cancer at the age of 37 in 2015 before he can publish the autobiographical account of his illness. The author's wife, the internist Lucy Goddard Kalanithi, sees the book through publication in January 2016. It remains #1 on the New York Times nonfiction bestseller list for 68 weeks, becomes a finalist for the Pulitzer Prize for auto/biography in 2017 and is translated into over 40 languages (lucykalanithi.com). The text chronicles how the promising young neurosurgeon, after a decade of training and ready to take up a position at one of the country's leading research universities, becomes a terminal patient himself.

The two-part narrative opens its prologue with the »obvious diagnosis« (3), before circling back through the previous year of denial (3-16). As the doctor-patient flips through the CT scan images, the narrator routinely comes to his conclusion: »Cancer, widely disseminated. I was a neurosurgical resident entering my final year of training. Over the last six years, I'd examined scores of such scans, on the off chance that some procedure might benefit the patient./ But this scan was different: it was my own« (3). In Kalanithi's text, as in many autopathographies and in medical realities (Couser 2004; Boyer 15-16; Maio 2020: 45-66), the diagnosis fundamentally puts into perspective a lived life, its unspoken assumptions and stabilizing convictions. It shakes up all coordinates in time, space, and relation which used to orient the patient in his environment. It catapults him into an intensively experienced present giving rise to conflicting emotions of fear, courage, devastation and happiness, as well as desires for meaningful agency, recognition, companionship, »for public life and civil society, for inclusion [and] purpose,« all of them frequently buried underneath a crowding plurality of daily routines and concerns (Solnit 1-10, here 6).

This fundamental shift in perspective is heightened here by the fact that the devastated patient is also a physician in the know. The formerly unspoken assumptions and stabilizing convictions of the doctor-patient Paul Kalanithi include research-driven and practically exercised world-class expertise in dealing with the issue of impending death in acute situations. These, too, are momentarily crushed: »Severe illness wasn't life-altering, it was life-shattering,« the narrator states. »My carefully planned and hard-won future no longer existed. Death, so familiar to me in my work, was now paying a personal visit. [...] yet nothing about it seemed recognizable. [...] as if a sandstorm had erased all traces of familiarity« (120-121). The patient's sensibilities thus question his own professional take on death. His take on statistics also becomes a different one as soon as he is required to look at his own life in terms of their logics: »The angst of facing mortality has no remedy in probability« (135). As conversant as he was as a doctor with his patients about impending death, he is at a loss, almost as much as them, when he, »so authoritative in a surgeon's coat« finds *himself* in the »meek« role of the patient (5, 6, see also 12, 180). As a patient, he experiences the lack of control that the protocols of his professional expertise had so efficiently covered over.

The memoir's »Part I: In Perfect Health I Begin« is dedicated to the build-up of the narrator-protagonist's medical expertise over two decades, and it connects that build-up with the protagonist's growing sense of ambition and his increasingly tight professional focus – both of them in line with his upbringing, especially with the role of his father. The narrator traces the protagonist's double interest in the philosophical and the scientific pursuit of existential questions concerning the interconnection of mind and brain, the human sense of identity and the biological framework enabling it. »I was driven less by achievement than by trying to understand, in earnest: What makes human life meaningful? I still felt literature provided the best account of the life of the mind, while neuroscience laid down the most elegant rules of the brain« (30-31). Having studied English at Stanford and History of medicine at Oxford, the protagonist decides to start medical school at Yale, even though he had never wanted to become a doctor. The example of his father, a cardiologist, had shown that doctors never had idle time and, for their families, were mostly absent (19-21). Believing that practicing medicine was the arena where »biology, morality, literature, and philosophy intersected[ed]« (41), however, Kalanithi specifically sought out »that direct experience of life-and-death questions,« because he felt that it »was essential to generating substantial moral opinions about them« (43).

The narrative raises significant points of critique concerning both the growing ambition of an intellectually curious young scientist and the medical profession. Going through the »medical rite of passage« of anatomical cadaver dissection, the young protagonist realizes that, for many students, the practice marks the »transformation of the somber, respectful student into the callous arrogant doctor« (44). He understands that it becomes an exercise in alienation:

> Anatomy lab, in the end, becomes less a violation of the sacred and more something that interferes with happy hour, and that realization discomfits. In our rare reflective moments, we were all silently apologizing to our cadavers, not because we sensed the transgression but because we did not. (49)

While understanding that »[s]eeing the body as matter and mechanism is the flip side to easing the most profound human suffering« (49), the narrator still insists that »Medical school sharpened my understanding of the relationship between meaning, life, and death. I saw the human relationality I had written about as an undergraduate realized in the doctor-patient relationship« (51). Kalanithi clearly started clinical work as an idealist. Seeking »to relieve concrete suffering, with patients, not abstractions, as [his] primary focus« (54, see also 77), he did not understand how much cutting-edge medicine is a strictly *physicalist* enterprise (Harrington 15-30) which would severely restrict his possibilities to ponder the relationship between meaning, life and death except in, precisely, the most *abstract* ways. His eyes on the prize of mastery, authority and perfection (71-72, 98), he nurses the ideal of the true doctor's »heroic spirit of responsibility amid blood and failure« (54). Given the placement of this retrospective account of learning after the brief introduction of the diagnosis in the prologue, there is considerable narrative irony mixed into the account of the student's earnest striving. In addition, the young doctor's ambition may be seen as closely tied not only to culturally ingrained US-American senses of progress and individual self-reliance, but also to masculinist notions of rugged individualism, mastery and invulnerability. In the account of his youth, the narrator critically cites his father's conviction that »[i]t's very easy to be number one: find the guy who is number one, and score one point higher than he does« as a »stony pronouncement« (21), typical for his father's »austere diktats« (20). He hadn't thought that he'd ever follow in those footsteps. Later, however, the protagonist's growing ambition becomes more and more pronounced. The narrator admits that, »a life spent in the space between« life and death was supposed to grant him »not merely a stage for compassionate action but an elevation of my own being,« a kind of transcendent escape from everyday materialism and pettiness (81). The narrator thus directly addresses the medical careerism which his idealism had merely covered. He further questions his high ideals when he speaks about the toll taken by up to a hundred hours of work per week, much of it highly intense: He was frequently exhausted (79), either losing focus on the relational foundation of his work (86, 96-97) or feeling vulnerable to crushing guilt if he kept it in place (98). He actually became inured to the suffering he had sought to ease (81). He understands that he had actually been acting as death's »ambassador« in his heroic drive to *save lives* rather than *protect identities* (87). The high medical calling of ›saving lives‹ becomes questionable to the narrator when it becomes untied from the patient's identity, when it attaches the medical doctor's dedication to a pulsing body rather than a comprehensive sense of a patient's life. Speaking about an admired colleague going through cancer treatment, the narrator even remarks: »How little do doctors understand the hells through which we put patients« (102). These more critical observations about the roles and interactions of doctors and patients that the narrator makes in part I of the memoir serve to anchor the text's critique of the unconditional US-American narrative of success that has been prepared in the prologue and is unfolded in »Part II: Cease Not till Death,« which again sets in with the diagnosis.

As a counterweight to the young neurosurgeon's striving for success, the text sheds critical light on the values that had supported the protagonist's professional ethos and in turn validates mortality, embodiment and vulnerability. Up until the diagnosis, and despite his philosophical interest in relationality and the mutually constitutive inter-connection between mind and body, the protagonist's social life had to take a backseat to the narrative of professional success that had scripted his adult life. He had dedicated all of his time, his physical and emotional resources, and his attention to his professional career, postponing his social life. At the end of his residency, he would soon reap the fruit of his strict work ethic: »At age thirty-six, I had reached the mountaintop; I could see the Promised Land [...]. I could see the tension in my back unwinding as my work schedule eased and life became more manageable. I could see myself finally becoming the husband I'd promised to be« (7). At this point of arrival almost within reach, he was not going to give in to the physical ailments he could easily read as serious symptoms. He was so much »determined to persevere for the next fifteen months, until residency ended« (6), that he even refrained from speaking to his wife about his suspected condition, which put considerable extra strain on a marriage bond already worn thin by years of multiple professional obligations. If he didn't speak about it, maybe it would go away: »Things are going to be okay« he tells himself and his estranged wife (9). Informed by these patterns of facing trouble with a potent mixture of denial and perseverance, the surgeon recently become patient can only take his unsought sense of embodiment as a sweeping failure. Even as a dying patient who accepts what is ahead of him, he thus finds himself unable to let go of the masculinist discursive power his professional position within the medical system, »with its unforgiving call to perfec-tion« (71), bestows upon him: »without that duty to care for the ill pushing me forward, I became an invalid« (125). So he returns to the operating room and to his role as a neurosurgical »maste[r] of many fields« (72) as soon as he possibly can, in order to be *in control* once more: »I was calling the shots« (159). For him, returning to work after 18 weeks meant returning to life, shedding the passivity connected to the role of the patient (150). And it meant betting on the most hopeful prognostication of 10 more years of life. But he quickly felt exhausted and the narrator admits that his work had become »joyless« (156). Nevertheless, he clings to the idea of »restor[ing] [his] life to its prior trajectory« (156). Reopening his job search, the narrator reports with con-siderable irony, he »could almost hear trumpets sounding a victory fanfare« (156). Subsequently the narrator rephrases this victory, confirming the sense of irony in his own hyperbolic pronouncement of triumph, as a desperate *need* to feel triumphant (165).

After conceding that living through terminal illness is a process which entails unstable evaluations, the narrator acknowledges his own »total denial« involved in his return to work (162): »I had striven with every ounce to restore my life to its precancer trajectory, trying to deny cancer any purchase on my life« (164). Recognizing the desperation and fear underlying his denial, he feels compelled to face »a strange and strained existence, challenging [him] to be neither blind to, nor bound by death's approach« (165). Faced with unknown territory under the sign of approaching death, he seeks to navigate a course between triumphant denial and desperate passivity. He seeks to fight for an inner space of rest rather than against his illness.

As I already indicated, the protagonist experiences this threatening change of perspective, his unsought embodiment and vulnerability, with considerable ambivalence. As his doctor Emma had told him, he needed to figure out what was important to him now. »Emma hadn't given me back my old identity. She'd protected my ability to forge a new one. And, finally, I knew I would have to« (166). In this process of attempting to think of his identity in different terms, the protagonist begins to see his profession critically and his »own hybris as a surgeon stood naked to [him] now« (166): it was his responsibility and power as a surgeon to perform successful crisis interventions, but he never solved those crises:

> the patient and family go on living – and things are never quite the same. A physician's words can ease the mind, just as the neurosurgeon's scalpel can ease a disease of the brain. Yet their uncertainties and morbidities, whether emotional or physical remain to be grappled with. (166)

Only as a patient does Kalanithi begin to question his professional position, which had, in the end, *not* allowed him to connect an interest in the body with an interest in the mind: Being a »leading actor« in *other* people's »medical dramas« (73) had been grand. But it did *not* allow him to be »*with* patients in their pivotal moments, I was merely *at* those pivotal moments. I observed a lot of suffering; worse, I became inured to it« (81, italics mine). Reaching back to his own interdisciplinary education, the narrator also relativizes science as *one* form of knowledge production that is ill understood if it is taken to include and thus cancel all others: transcendent revelation, literary or philosophical knowledge production. The scientific »view from nowhere« has, as he admits in his literary view from a socio-culturally and affectively situated standpoint, its own blind spots:[9]

> Science may provide the most useful way to organize empirical, reproducible data, but its power to do so is predicated on its inability to grasp the most central aspects of human life: hope, love, hate, beauty, envy, honor, weakness, striving, suffering, virtue.

> Between these core passions and scientific theory, there will always be a gap. No system of thought can contain the fullness of human experience. (170)

---

9   For a heuristic juxtaposition of the scientific »view from nowhere« and the literary »view from somewhere« see Kley 2016.

The narrator concludes:

> In the end, it cannot be doubted that each of us can only see part of the picture. The
> doctor sees one, the patient another, the engineer a third, the economist a fourth, the
> pearl diver a fifth, the alcoholic a sixth, the cable guy a seventh, the sheep farmer an
> eighth, the Indian beggar a ninth, the pastor a tenth. Human knowledge is never con-
> tained in one person. It grows from the relationships we create between each other and
> the world, and still it is never complete. (172)

Guided by this idea of the inherent imperfectability of any one perspective, he is able,
during the subsequent relapse and feeling weak, to allow his need for control to ease and
make room for a sense of conscious and sensitive acceptance of the wealth of the life he
has left. His wife confirms, in her posthumous epilogue to the text, how he consciously
enjoyed the support of friends and family and »let himself be open and vulnerable, let
himself be comforted« (219). She confirms that, in contradistinction to the strenuous
time of denial during the year before the diagnosis, her husband remained in sensitive
relation to her and to his environment. »Even while terminally ill, Paul was fully alive;
despite physical collapse, he remained vigorous, open, full of hope not for an unlikely
cure but for days that were full of purpose and meaning« (219). Kalanithi experiences
the birth of his daughter, in particular, in ways which affirm and enrich his sense of
embodiment and vulnerability: »Feeling her weight in one arm, and gripping Lucy's
hand with the other, the possibilities of life emanated before us« (195). Abandoning
frantic activity and ambition, Kalanithi's sense of time also changes, as he seems to heed
the Fulke Greville line he quotes at the beginning of the book: »Reader! Then make
time, while you be,/ But steps to your eternity« (ix). He adopts what he calls a »tor-
toiselike approach. I plod, I ponder. Some days, I simply persist« (197). His sense of time
changes significantly: Future orientation and delayed gratification wash away into an
expansive immediate present.

Needing a communicative examination of death and needing to be present in time
are, as Corinna Caduff suggests, effects of the permanent stress experienced by working
generations in late modern high-performance societies. Where predominant values
tightly circle around performance and efficiency, death is the most radical disruption of
›normal life‹ and facing mortality the most radical form of slowing down. Slowing
down is a practice frequently evoked but little practiced with any consequence in high
performance cultures. It is a symptom of a time that is experienced as passing too fast.
As Caduff explains:

> In order to develop and embed a consciousness of death, a society must enable the
> experience of present-ness, the experience of ›having time,‹ of ›being in time.‹
> Therefore, new figurations of death might be rooted in our longing for adjourning,

pausing, lingering – in order to experience and become conscious of time. In order to become evanescent (239-241, here 241, translation mine).[10]

Along these lines Kalanithi's text substantiates the connection I see between the serious contemplation of mortality and a profound criticism of late modern forms of economic and social life. Saturated in this new conscious sense of time slowed down, Part II of the memoir ends with the narrator-protagonist addressing a letter to his daughter: »you filled a dying man's days with a sated joy, a joy unknown to me in all prior years, a joy that does not hunger for more and more but rests, satisfied. In this time, right now, that is an enormous thing« (199). The text thus offers a perspective from which it becomes possible to understand that the ideology inscribed in the need to ›fight the disease as an enemy‹ makes it impossible to *live with* the disease. Allowing personal recognition and support are major steps in letting go of the combative take that underlies the desperate need, encouraged by a thoroughly economized hospital system and a competitive culture of achievement, to repair the body to a previous condition. As Kalanithi undergoes this transformation, he is enabled, under first class medical treatment and in the midst of a »death-avoidant culture« (215), to develop new, poignantly meaningful conceptions of a life worth living with cancer.[11]

4. Death-avoidance and new visibilities: Western attitudes toward death

As Philippe Ariès has explained in his 1973 classic study *Western Attitudes Toward Death*, confrontation with death has been spatially and emotionally marginalized in Western societies since the late nineteenth century. And, as the psychologist Pauline

---

10 The German original reads: »Um ein Todesbewusstsein aktuell zu verankern, muss eine Gesellschaft die Erfahrung von Gegenwärtigkeit ermöglichen, die Erfahrung von ›Zeit haben‹, ›in der Zeit sein‹. Dementsprechend scheinen die neuen Figurationen des Todes nicht zuletzt begründet in unserer Sehnsucht danach, endlich einmal auszusetzen, einzuhalten und zu verweilen – um Zeit wieder erfahren und begreifen zu können. Um vergänglich zu werden« (239-241, here 241).

11 The fact that the dying patient reconsiders long abandoned Christian values of »sacrifice, redemption, forgiveness« for their compelling stand »against blind determinism« (171) confirms the historian Anne Harrington's claim that the various branches of current mind-body medicine and their critique of a strictly physicalist medical system gain much of their authority from recourse to older religious traditions (245-247). A second set of concerns she identifies as amplifying mind-body medicine's »efforts to talk coherently about what it means to be human« (254) are cultural anxieties about the costs of modernization in general and about material prosperity, masculinity, weakening family and community bonds, in particular (246-247). These concerns surface strongly in Kalanithi's text. For an up-to-date anthropological conception of a trans-religious *ars moriendi* see Leget.

Boss has shown in her work over the past 20 years, the American nation in particular, a nation invested in imagining itself in control of its own and other nations' fate, suffers from what she calls »ambiguous loss« – from individually and collectively unaddressed grief. Boss attributes US-American ambiguous loss to the history of slavery and racism, the Civil War, the history of immigration, the wars in Korea, Vietnam and the middle East, 9/11 and last but not least the Corona pandemic – all of which sent strong and lasting senses of mortification across a country highly invested in making, doing and success. Biomedical development since the end of WWII also extends the repression of death in ambivalent ways: on the one hand, people who enjoy unhindered access to the modern medical system grow much older and encounter death later and less frequently in their lives than earlier generations. But while people in high tech cultures grow older, the experience of aging and dying becomes a stage of life in its own right and it remains under-examined. Speaking about the medical system, the surgeon and author Atul Gawande explains:

> Our reluctance to honestly examine the experience of aging and dying has increased the harm we inflict on people and denied them the basic comforts they most need. Lacking a coherent view of how people might live successfully all the way to their end, we have allowed our fates to be controlled by the imperatives of medicine, technology and strangers. (9).

Sharon Kaufman confirms in her study of how hospitals shape the end of life in the US, that the hospital has become, since the 1980s, the primary place and institution where, in high tech and high-performance cultures, spatially and psychologically repressed encounters with mortality return with a vengeance in all their personal and cultural ambivalence.

Biomedical progress has normalized longevity and stabilized medicine as a con-sumer product and practice. It has also brought with it enormous medical and personal complications and frequently a protraction of the process of dying a ›natural‹ death. Under current biomedical conditions, dying frequently becomes a significant and considerably long phase of life in its own right (Carr). In the late 1960s, the intensive care concept of brain death was introduced. Since the 1980s and up to this very day, the concept has been connected to controversial and ongoing public debates around the definition of death both in the US and in Europe. These debates have, together with the increase in longevity and the occurrence of degenerative diseases, contributed to making death and dying a frequent topic of public discussion. In late industrial societies, death thus becomes a public issue of debate at a time when traditional Christian rituals of mourning have lost authority as a widely shared practice.[12] However, these debates hardly contribute to clarifying how we live content and in dignity all the way to our end.

In line with Kaufman's claim that dying in late capitalist societies predominantly takes place in hospitals, Kalanithi explains that »the questions intersecting life, death, and meaning, questions that all people face at some point, usually arise in a medical context« (70). And he adds that their encounter and address is at least as much a *philosophical* as a biological exercise, emphasizing that the medical system produces or exacerbates problematics it is ill-equipped to address with its own resources (Gawande). Kalanithi finds himself needing, in addition to medical treatment, *words*, i.e. a non-scientific form of abstraction, to go forward:

> Lost in a featureless wasteland of my own mortality, and finding no traction in the reams of scientific studies, intercellular molecular pathways, and endless curves of survival statistics, I began reading literature again: [...] – anything by anyone who had ever written about mortality. I was searching for a vocabulary with which to make sense of death, to find a way to begin defining myself and inching forward again. The privilege of direct experience had let me away from literary and academic work, yet now I felt that to understand my own direct experiences, I would have to translate them back into language. (148-149)

With its reach for language, indirection and perspective, Kalanithi's text is an instance of a larger cultural formation insisting on an address and examination of mortality.

Death as a new *cultural* topic began to grow with the development of »personal accounts of illness and dying« after World War II, as the medical profession transformed with the wide availability of antibiotics and vaccines, turning its primary focus from infectious to chronic diseases (Jurecic 4-17). As the health system persistently medicalized human lives from birth to death, patients also became more active medical consumers seeking treatment for conditions previously not considered medical. Many patients, however, also became alienated from the system. Antipsychiatry and the women's health movement picked up on this growing sense of alienation among patients and helped initiate the development of the political or activist patient. Jurecic cites six publications which discursively paved the way for this development and for an increasing number of personal illness narratives resisting the capitalist medicalization of life and the objectification of the patient.[13] These narratives carve out space for the

---

12 Clearly, and in particular in the US, there are significant fundamentalist counter movements, but it seems safe to say that the loss of a widely shared Christian faith leaves a vacuum in its wake which calls for new and sustainable modes of addressing experiences of death and grief.

13 On the medicalization of life and death and the medical quest for control of human bodies see Ehrenreich and Gawande.

reflection of existential questions connected to personal health issues that do not have room in medical institutions, which are systematically, and with considerable success, focused on the eradication of disease.

The six trailblazing publications identified by Jurecic are the Swiss-American psychiatrist Elisabeth Kübler-Ross' account of the five stages of grief, *On Death and Dying* (1969); the first edition of the feminist medical bible *Our Bodies Ourselves* (1970); the Christian ethicist Paul Ramsay's first account of bioethics, *The Patient as Person: Explorations in Medical Ethics* (1970); the Austrian-American theologian and critic of progress Ivan Illich's *The Medical Nemesis: The Expropriation of Health*; the American director, author and social critic Susan Sontag's *Illness as Metaphor* (1977) which fought the stigmatization of cancer patients; and finally the journalist Norman Cousins' *Anatomy of an Illness as Perceived by the Patient: Reflections on Healing and Regeneration* (1979). The tide of personal illness narratives in the wake of these publications swelled with the narrative negotiations of the AIDS crisis in the 1980s and 1990s, which produced, in a variety of genres and media, »a thunderous cacophony of voices« by patients, their relatives and friends, journalists, medical personnel, and novelists about »loss, sorrow, struggle, rage, and redemption or its absence« (Jurecic 2, 8-10), i.e. about »matters of concern« (Latour) not addressed in medical discourse.

Since then, cultural productions of the past three or four decades in all media frequently address death, illness, dying and bereavement ushering in a »new cultural visibility« of death in transatlantic cultural geographies (Macho/Marek 9-21, Caduff, Anderson).[14] At the end of the 20th century, digital and digitally organized practices of commemoration emerge.[15] The concept of ›digital immortality‹ as well as social debates around digital legacy also gain traction. With digitalization, the understanding and structuring of the experience of death, which is connected to a set of people, particular times, places, as well as culturally specific objects and symbols, also assumes new shape and form (Cutter 105-120, Caduff 173-202). Altogether, this new cultural visibility of death is in part a reaction to, and it collides with, the social denial and repression of death, dying, and mourning I have addressed at the outset of this section. It indicates an ongoing recalibration of the social significance of death.

---

[14]   Cursory examples are photographs like those by Sue Fox, films (like *Death Becomes Her*), TV-series (like *Six Feet Under*, *Dead Like Me*, *C.S.I.*, and more recently *The Good Place* or *After Life*), Comics and Graphic Novels (like those by Alison Bechdel and Tom Hart), Games, Performances, international exhibitions (like the anatomist Gunter von Hagens' *Body Worlds*), autobiographies, novels. Additionally, the ongoing process of digitalization has opened up new ›thana-technological‹ spaces for an individualized processing of death, dying, loss, and grief.

[15]   One example is the practice of conducting non-commercial discussion groups on death, the so-called death cafés which, starting from London, have spread internationally since 2010 (www.deathcafe.com).

The internet and, in particular, social media also further amplify the production of multiplied, multimedia and frequently relational or collaborative versions of illness narratives, both offering visibility and enabling selection and surveillance (Bolaki 211-221). Illness narratives may seem self-indulgent or utilitarian in their demand for empathetic engagement with the ›victim‹ of disease. I want to insist, however, with Jurecic and Bolaki that these representations' media-specific formal and generic constructions and their staging of conflicting ideologies »continue to test the possibility that a narrative will do meaningful work in the world« (Jurecic 11, Bolaki 220-221).[16] I choose to join those whose work on illness narratives and representations of dying and bereavement seeks to be both critically discerning and empathetic, employing both hermeneutically suspicious and reparative modes of reading – in order to identify the what and the how of the cultural work they perform. This kind of critical work rejects a deeply problematic divide between embodied everyday experience and unaffected cultural criticism, between the emotional and the rational, between ethics and aesthetics – without assuming they are the same.[17]

5. Literary knowledge production: a conclusion

When Breath Becomes Air presents the medical hospital as a social space that is inherently ill-equipped for the negotiation of the personally and culturally contradictory process of dying that, in late capitalist consumer societies and since the 1980s, predominantly takes place in its confines. Recent journalistic work (Ehrenreich, Gawande, Mikich) and research in medical history (Illich), medical sociology (Kaufman) as well as medical ethics (President's Council on Bioethics) systematically explores these weaknesses of late capitalist societies' high tech medical systems: they are geared towards the control of disease and cost at the expense of a clear-eyed and emotionally supportive view of life's end. Only on the fringes of the medical system, in medical ethics and the recently developed branch of palliative care, does a more humble but strongly supportive take on the human body and both its physical and mental needs take hold (Maio 2011, Maio 2020, Student 2004).

When Breath Becomes Air is a paradigmatic example for the contribution literary forms of knowledge production might provide in a discursive field which, in late

---

16   See also Kainradel/Kriebernegg, Kainradl et al. and Oró-Piqueras/Wohlmann.
17   In addition to the critics already mentioned, I include Jessica Restaino in this open ›we‹. She allows the conceptual walls »between the personal, the academic and the analytic« to become permeable (9). »What happens when we refuse to operate in only one area at a time,« she asks, opening up her work on a friend's death to the experience of *not* knowing – in order to transform what it means to write, to do research, and to be a friend (9-11).

capitalist societies, is securely framed by medical, economic, legal and residual religious protocols. Literary knowledge production has many facets; here I am primarily concerned with »matters of concern« (Latour) that are more poignantly – and with more searching specificity – discussed in literary writing than in medical, care, religious or insurance protocols (Kley 2016, Kley 2018: 9-14, Bolaki 11). With the resources of literary expression (a tragic story and a compelling narrative voice) and equipped with the powers of the business of literature (which place a well-pitched book internationally in both the prestigious and the popular limelight), *When Breath Becomes Air* provides a much-needed perspective on death and hospital culture. It highlights the fundamental contradictions between a thoroughly economized high tech hospital system and the needs of terminally ill patients who require that systems' services. It thus juxtaposes the hospital system's efficient control of cost and disease as well as its masculinist notions of hierarchy and command with the suffering body's need for recognition and physical as well as emotional support. This juxtaposition indicates that the hospital system needs to make room for the perspective it marginalizes in order to *respond* to the needs of the ill body.[18]

By deflating masculinist notions of control and by exploring the alternative qualities needed to face mortality, *When Breath Becomes Air* attends to the issue of human vulnerability the hospital system exacerbates but cannot attend to with its own resources (Kaufman, Gawande). With its literary address of the experience of dying, *When Breath Becomes Air* thus offers an important form of alternative knowledge production to currently dominant medical, care, insurance and legal discourses on vulnerability, mortality and death. At a larger scale the text articulates a critique of late capitalist high tech societies' need for control and their heightened demands on the individual's resources of time, creativity, flexibility, and commitment. Deflating those urgencies, culturally coded masculine, healthy and strong, the text implies the existential need for the strengthening of relationality and solidarity. Under the sign of death, the habituated economic logics of augmentation quickly become unreal. The text thus exposes a longing for a different quality of relation to the world; a relation to the world that is attuned to the body and to the relational nature of knowledge, enquiry, friendship and life; a relation to the world that may »resonate,« as the sociologist

---

[18] In his first study of literary narrative as a resource for medical sociology, *The Wounded Storyteller*, Frank also connects the suffering body's need with the hospital system's deficits and the vital communicative function of stories: »administrative systems [...] cannot take suffering into account because they are abstracted from the needs of bodies. When the body's vulnerability and pain are kept in the foreground [through the telling of witness accounts], a new social ethic is required« (2013: 146). Frank suggests that the »pedagogy of suffering« (2013: 145), which illness witness accounts may provide, significantly contribute to the development of a »new, multivocal clinical ethic« (2013: 147), which seeks to make sure the hospital system is better oriented toward the patient as a person than it has been.

Hartmut Rosa would have it, with the needs of individuals and groups (Rosa 2021, Rosa 2018). A both humble and pleasurable relation to the world that is attuned to the needs of bodies and a broadly inclusive »ethics of vulnerability,« as Martin Schnell develops it at the crossroads of philosophy and nursing, does not have a systematic place wherever growth imperatives are prevalent. Therefore, late capitalist societies are in acute need for artistic reflection and imaginary arrangement of such ethics and relations to the world as *When Breath Becomes Air* enacts it. The text prompts its readers to expand and defer seemingly self-evident notions of ›normal life‹. Dodging the pervasive rhetoric of personal development and the heroic overcoming of pain and grief, the text articulates the contours of a shaken and fundamentally uncertain life and imagines it with all its contradictions as a volatile point of reference.

Works Cited

Primary Source

Kalanithi, Paul (2016): *When Breath Becomes Air.* New York: Random House.

Research Literature

Ariès, Philippe (1973): *Western Attitudes Toward Death: From the Middle Ages to the Present.* Trans. Patricia M. Ranum. London: Marion Boyars.

Anderson, Inga (2018): *Bilder guter Trauer: Neue Sichtbarkeiten der Trauer in der Psychologie, Philosophie und Fotografie.* München: Fink.

Banerjee, Mita (2011): *Medical Humanities in American Studies: Life Writing, Narrative Medicine, and the Power of Autobiography.* Heidelberg: Winter.

Berlant, Lauren (2011): *Cruel Optimism.* Durham, NC: Duke University Press.

Bielefeldt, Heiner/Frewer, Andreas/Osgathe, Christoph/Welsh, Caroline (eds.) (2017): *Autonomie und Menschenrechte am Lebensende: Grundlagen, Erfahrungen, Reflexionen aus der Praxis.* Bielefeld: transcript.

Bolaki, Stella (2016): *Illness as Many Narratives: Arts, Medicine and Culture.* Edinburgh: Edinburgh University Press.

Boss, Pauline (1999): *Ambiguous Loss: Learning to Live with Unresolved Grief.* Cambridge: Harvard University Press.

Broeckling, Ulrich (2015). *The Entrepreneurial Self: Fabricating a New Type of Subject.* Los Angeles: Sage Publictions.

Butler, Judith/Gambetti, Zeynep/Sabsay, Leticia (2016): »Rethinking Vulnerability and Resistance.« In: Butler, Judith et al. (eds.): *Vulnerability in Resistance.* Durham: Duke UP, pp. 12-27.

Caduff, Corinna (2013): *Szenen des Todes: Essays.* Basel: Lenos.

Carr, Deborah/Luth, Elizabeth A. (2019): »*Well-Being at the End of Life.*« *Annual Review of Sociology* 45, pp. 515-534. https://doi.org/10.1146/annurev-soc-073018-022524. Accessed July 10, 2022.

Charon, Rita (2006): *Narrative Medicine. Honoring the Stories of Illness.* New York: Oxford University Press.

Couser, G. Thomas (1991): »Autopathography: Women, Illness, and Life-writing.« In: *a/b: Auto/biography Studies,* vol. 6, no. 1, pp. 65-75.

Couser, G. Thomas (1997): *Recovering Bodies. Illness, Disability, and Life Writing.* Madison: University of Wisconsin Press.

Couser, G. Thomas (2004): *Vulnerable Subjects: Ethics and Life Writing.* Ithaca/London: Cornell University Press.

Couser, G. Thomas (2016): »Body Language: Illness, Disability and Life Writing.« In: *Life Writing,* vol. 13, no. 1, pp. 3-10.

Cutter, Mary Ann G. (2019): *Death: A Reader.* Notre Dame: U of Notre Dame P, 2019.

Ehrenreich, Barbara (2018): *Natural Causes: Life, Death and The Illusion of Control.* New York: Twelve.

Frank, Arthur W. (2013): *The Wounded Storyteller: Body, Illness, and Ethics.* 1995. 2nd ed. Chicago: University of Chicago Press.

Frank, Arthur W. (2010): *Letting Stories Breathe: A Socio-Narratology.* Chicago: University of Chicago Press.

Gawande, Atul. (2014): *Being Mortal: Medicine and What Matters in the End.* New York: Metropolitan Books.

Gergen, Kenneth J. (2009): *Relational Being: Beyond Self and Community.* New York: Oxford University Press.

Gilman, Sander L. (1988): *Disease and Representation: Images of Illness from Madness to AIDS.* Ithaca/London: Cornell University Press.

Gilbert, Sandra M. (2006): *Death's Door: Modern Dying and the Ways We Grieve.* New York: Norton.

Gómez-Vírseda, Carlos/de Maeseneer, Yves/Gastmans, Chris (2019): »Relational autonomy: what does it mean and how is it used in end-of-life care? A systematic review of argument-based ethics literature.« In: *BMC medical ethics,* vol. 20, no. 1. 26.10.2019. doi:10.1186/s12910-019-0417-3. Accessed July 10, 2022.

Harrington, Anne (2008): *The Cure Within: A History of Mind-Body Medicine.* New York: Norton.

Illich, Ivan (1995): *Limits to Medicine.* London: Marion Boyars.

Jurecic, Ann (2012): *Illness As Narrative.* Pittsburgh, PA: University of Pittsburgh Press.

Kainradl, Anna-Christina/Kriebernegg, Ulla (2021): »Bad News? Literarische Care-Beziehungen als Utopien des Alter(n)s.« In: Gronemeyer, Reimer/Schuchter, Patrick/Wegleitner, Klaus (eds.): *Care – Vom Rande betrachtet. In welcher Gesellschaft wollen wir leben und sterben?* Bielefeld: transcript, pp. 97-114.

Kainradl, Anna-Christina/Kriebernegg, Ulla/Trinkaus, Eva-Maria et al. (eds.) (2021): *Alter(n) und Pflege gemeinsam neu denken: Interdisziplinäre Perspektiven aus Wissenschaft und Praxis.* Wien: facultas.

Kaufman, Sharon R. (2005): ... *And A Time To Die: How Hospitals Shape the End of Life*. New York: Scribner.

Kley, Antje (2016): »Literary Knowledge Production and the Natural Sciences in the US.« In: Knewitz, Simone/Klöckner, Christian/Sielke, Sabine (eds.): *Knowledge Landscapes North America*. Heidelberg: Winter, pp. 153-177.

Kley, Antje (2018). »What Literature Knows: An Introduction.« In: Kley, Antje/Merten, Kai (eds.): *What Literature Knows: Forays into Literary Knowledge Production*. Heidelberg: Winter, pp. 9-25.

Kunow, Rüdiger (2018): *Material Bodies: Biology and Culture in the United States*. Heidelberg: Winter.

Latour, Bruno (2004): »Why Has Critique Run out of Steam? From Matters of Fact to Matters of Concern.« In: *Critical Inquiry*, vol. 30, Winter 2004, pp. 225-248.

Macho, Thomas/Marek, Kristin (eds.) (2007): *Die Neue Sichtbarkeit des Todes*. München: Fink.

Maio, Giovanni (2020): *Den Kranken Menschen Verstehen: Für Eine Medizin Der Zuwendung*. 2nd ed. Freiburg: Herder.

Maio, Giovanni (ed.) (2011): *Abschaffung des Schicksals? Menschsein Zwischen Gegebenheit des Lebens und Medizin-Technischer Gestaltbarkeit*. Freiburg: Herder.

Leget, Carlo (2017): *Art of Living, Art of Dying: Spiritual Care for a Good Death*. London/ Philadelphia: Jessica Kingsley Publishers.

Mikich, Sonia (2013): *Warum Uns der Medizinbetrieb Krank Macht*. München: Bertelsmann.

Oró-Piqueras, Maricel/Wohlmann, Anita (eds.) (2015): *Serializing Age: Aging and Old Age in TV Series*. Bielefeld: transcript.

President's Council On Bioethics (2003): *Beyond Therapy: Biotechnology and The Pursuit of Happiness*. New York: Regan.

Restaino, Jessica (2019): *Surrender: Feminist Rhetoric and Ethics in Love and Illness*. Carbondale: Southern Illinois University Press.

Rosa, Hartmut (2021): *Resonance: A Sociology of Our Relationship to the World*. Medford, MA: Polity Press.

Rosa, Hartmut (2018): *The Uncontrollability of the World*. Medford, MA: Polity Press.

Schnell, Martin W. (2017): *Ethik im Zeichen Vulnerabler Personen: Leiblichkeit – Endlichkeit – Nichtexklusivität*. Weilerswist: Velbrück Wissenschaft.

Solnit, Rebecca (2009): *A Paradise Built in Hell: The Extraordinary Communities That Arise in Disaster*. New York: Penguin.

Further Sources

Baker, Douglas E. (2019): »Death Becomes Us.« *Tenth Presbyterian Church:* https://www.tenth. org/resource-library/tenth-presses/death-becomes-us/. Accessed May 22, 2022.

Boyer, Anne (2019): *The Undying. Pain, Vulnerablity, Mortality, Medicine, Art, Time, Dreams, Data, Exhaustion, Cancer and Care*. New York: Farrar, Straus and Giroux.

Butler, Judith/Yancy, George (2020): »Interview by George Yancy: Mourning is a Political Act Amid the Pandemic and its Disparities (Republication).« Springer Link Online / *Bioethical*

Enquiry (2020): https://link.springer.com/article/10.1007/s11673-020-10043-6. Accessed May 22, 2022.

Ensler, Eve (2013): *In the Body of the World*. New York: Metropolitan Books.

Kalanithi, Lucy (n.d.): »Homepage.« Lucy Kalanithi Homepage: https://lucykalanithi.com/. Accessed May 22, 2022.

Skjolsvik, Pamela (2015): *Death Becomes Us*. North Charleston: CreateSpace Independent Publishing Platform.

Student, Johann-Christoph (ed.) (2004): *Sterben, Tod und Trauer: Handbuch für Begleitende*. Freiburg: Herder.

Rüdiger Heinze

Cognitive Confusions and Critical Misapprehensions

Henry James's »The Real Thing«

ABSTRACT: This essay uses principles and concepts of cognitive psychology and the context of 19th-century visual culture to show that the narrator of Henry James's »The Real Thing« (1892) is an unreliable narrator – a point which has been made before – not primarily because his judgments are incongruous with those of an implied author (a troubled concept in itself) and reader (as has been argued by critics so far) but rather because the manner in which he perceives and judges is so much d'accord with the way humans tend to perceive and judge: by heuristic processes of selection, projection and generalization. As I will further argue, these processes of cognition also have serious ethical repercussions – a point mostly overlooked so far.

KEYWORDS: Henry James; visual culture; cognitive cultural studies; psychology; narrative theory

> It is the spectator, and not life, that art really mirrors.
> (Oscar Wilde in his preface to The Picture of Dorian Gray)

> [F]or the critics, as for the governess, the characters and events around which the narrative turns, and turns again, evoke a profound unease in the face of epistemological as well as ethical uncertainty, and hence a tendency to impose univocal order and sense on language that strongly resists such acts of force.
> The criticism that has emerged around James's tale is often as much a record of efforts to quell that anxiety as it is an attempt to understand a story that consistently defies such efforts.
> (Esch & Warren, preface to The Turn of the Screw, xi)

I. Introduction: No Larger Than Life[1]

Henry James's short story »The Real Thing« (1892) begins with the narrator recounting a moment when the porter's wife announces »A gentleman – with a lady, sir« (James 1963: 229). The announcement of the gentleman and the lady triggers a »vision of sitters« – the first mistake on the side of the narrator, as it turns out. After their introduction and the removal of the initial misunderstanding – the »sitters« (who

---

1 I would like to thank the reviewers, whose suggestions and comments have significantly improved the essay.

would pay *him*) actually want to be »models« (who would be paid *by him*) – the narrator is »disappointed; for in the pictorial sense I had immediately *seen* them. I had seized their type–I had already settled what I would do with it« (231). This early deceptive impression is repeatedly corroborated in the course of the story by numerous conjectures such as »It was odd how quickly I was sure of everything that concerned them« (235). Given that the narrator has never before seen his sitters, the Monarchs, and that he has never been in contact with »their type« (»I seemed not to know any of the people he and his wife had known« (242)) we have to deduce that he cannot realistically seize their type at all – at least not from firsthand experience.[2] As it turns out, his claims are failures of cognition and judgment – failures that are never fully remedied: the narrative situation sets up a contrast between an experiencing I and an experienced I. The latter seems vaguely cognizant of the cognitive confusions which »got [him] into a second-rate trick« (258), but he never scrutinizes the causes of these confusions and consecutively readapts his percepts. His cognizance of that »second-rate trick« may count as partial insight, but he still blames this »trick« on the Monarchs without acknowledging his own failure. It is ironic that he comes to his insight in part by relying on the judgment of his friend Jack, who knows even less about the Monarchs and is apparently a bad/amateur painter (251), something which the narrator explicitly scorns earlier on (236f). To double the irony, the narrator conclusively purports to value memory so highly that he is »content to have paid the price–for the memory« (258). Yet it is his non-existent previous experience and the resulting impossibility of a memory (how could he remember something which never happened?) which lead him to his rather rash cognitive claims in the first place.

All this makes him an unreliable narrator; that much is uncontroversial. Catherine Vieilledent, Samuel Ludwig, Stuart Burrows, Michael Butter and others all have observed that the story »opens with a moment of vision that proves deceptive« (Burrows 255), that the narrator is not an acute observer because he is repeatedly mistaken, and that the text »suggests certain shortcomings of his ability to represent reality« (Ludwig 171). Far fewer critics, however, follow up on this: the narrator is unreliable not so much because his judgments are incongruous with those of conceivable readers or the wider implicit rules and norms of the storyworld but rather because the manner in which he perceives and judges is *so much d'accord* with the way humans tend to perceive and judge: by heuristic processes of selection, projection and generalization.

As John Armstrong has shown at length and in detail in his work on Henry James, phenomenology, and cognition, James is a »phenomenological writer«. In his groundbreaking *Phenomenology of Henry James* (1983), Armstrong writes: »James's heroes and heroines have dramas because they have impressions; indeed, their dramas

---

[2]   As Fiorenzo Iuliano points out, the sitters are aptly named Monarch (Iuliano 2019) – and how many people can boast to actually know monarchs from firsthand experience?

are their impressions. And he tells their stories by relating the impressions of observers, registers, or reflectors« (1983, 3; see also 37ff). In a more recent contribution, Armstrong argues that James shows and makes us aware of »the constructive powers of cognitive pattern-making that we ordinarily do not notice in everyday perception« (140). This pattern formation is a »temporal process of projecting expectations that are then *modified, refined, or overturned*« (2018, 141; emphasis mine). It would therefore be misleading to assume that the narrator's ›failure‹ of cognition suggests the availability of a perfect cognition, on the contrary; cognitive confusions and misapprehensions are an essential part of how humans make sense of the world and for this, the narrator cannot seriously be faulted. But it is when a lack of self-awareness and self-reflexivity – in other words: the unwillingness or inability to *modify, reflect*, and, if necessary, *overturn* one's temporary expectations, impressions, and formed patterns[3]– combines with these all too human misapprehensions and consequently leads to hasty attributions, stereotypes and prejudices, that questions of epistemological and narrative reliability and, most importantly and seriously, moral judgment enter. It is this last aspect of ethics and morality that is, I argue, regularly overlooked.[4]

Coincidentally, ironically, and testament to Henry James's mastery, we as readers run the danger of replicating the narrator's failures of judgment/cognition. As Sam Whitsitt argues, this is due to the fact that the story tells several, overlapping yet contradictory stories at once, so that the narrative »differ[s] with itself« and the narrator is »split, not into two—but into a differing within the same« (306). Many critics, he explains, take the artist's word for it and try to disambiguate[5] at all costs; »they assume that the narrator who tells us about the transformative powers of art has not in turn transformed that very story« (305). However, »whether the artist teaches a lesson to a pair of would-be models, or the would-be models teach a lesson to the artist remains an open question, not in spite of but because critics have apparently felt compelled to decide the issue one way or another« (304). In this respect, the story carries the same characteristics that Deborah Esch and Jonathan Warren ascribe to James's hallmark example of narrative, epistemological and ethical unreliability, *The Turn of the Screw*.

---

3   As Whitsitt puts it, the narrator »does not ever *master[.]* this [initial] mistake, this fracture, this gap« between the cognition of the experiencing I and the reflecting experienced I (309; emphasis in the original).

4   Theoretically, one could argue that humans are always already unreliable and that subsequently there cannot be an entirely reliable human narrator. While this is *generally* true (and also truistic), it ignores that there is an entire, epistemologically complex spectrum of degrees and facets of reliability.

5   »Disambiguation« shall be used in the logical sense introduced by Jeremy Bentham, i.e. the fixing of the various possible senses and meanings of an ambiguous term in order to determine one specific meaning.

Considering the story's cultural historical background, the cognitive confusions do not come as a surprise: the 19th century, and particularly the second half, witnessed an increasing and insistent orientation towards visuality, an »increasing freedom of spectacular display« as well as an »increasing awareness of the ubiquity of surveillance« (Brosch xi). Conventional visual codes were destabilized through ever more quickly developing mass media and technological novelties (Brosch 2) culminating in what Renate Brosch calls a »crisis of seeing.« If we follow the cognitive psychological hypothesis that perception and cognition are influenced by cultural determinants (Bierhoff 262ff; Armstrong calls humans »bio-social hybrids;« 2019, 133ff), and add to this Lakoff's postulation that symbolic models pair with cognitive models (154) through the »*structuring* of experience« (302; emphasis in the original), then »James's excessive use of the observer in his texts can be seen as a structural analogy to the cultural emphasis on the visual« (Brosch xii).

Moreover, his emphasis on processes of human cognition and their inherent pitfalls and shortcomings, disruptions and failures can also be seen as a structural analogy to the increasing heterogeneity, multiplication, ambiguation and destabilization of visual codes and human cognition at the end of the 19th century, lasting until today. If »seeing typically involves categorizing« (Lakoff 127), then a crisis of seeing also effects a crisis of categorizing and inevitably (as categories perform a crucial function in the formation of our judgments) a crisis of ethics and morality.[6] Racism, classism, ableism and various other forms of discrimination are all based on categorization and, to varying degrees, visuality.

By analogy, one could say that when reading »The Real Thing«, one executes cognitive processes akin to those activated upon looking at a Phenakistiscope or a Wheatstone stereoscope (Crary 28-31), the significant difference being semantic rather than visual confluence. Although we can never see any of the pictures and illustrations described and referred to in the story (it is after all only one semiotic system, a pro-

---

[6] These cognitive problems are among the reasons the introspective psychology of William James and others was largely ignored in the US around the turn of the last century: it produced contradictory and often practically irrelevant results. William James writes on knowing (identified as cognition) that »[f]inding a world before him which he [the psychologist] cannot but believe that he knows, and setting himself to study his own past thoughts, or someone else's thoughts, of what he believes to be the same world; he cannot but conclude that those other thoughts know it after their fashion even as he knows it after his« (216). Thus, »the waking minds of our fellows and our own minds know the same external world« (218). The experimental refutation of these claims provided a fertile ground for the repudiation of this version of cognitive psychology by behaviorism. The latter restricted itself to the observation of observable behavior and did not attempt to hypothesize mental processes. It was only after the limits of behaviorism crystallized and when a change in methodology and new research into computer sciences and artificial intelligence provided good models that cognitive psychology experienced a revival (Anderson 20).

totypical example of ekphrasis), we inevitably imagine them: »Wir gestalten räumlich-bildliche Strukturen beim Verstehen sprachlicher Kunstwerke, und wir entwerfen sprachliche Kontexte beim sukzessiven Lesen von bildlichen Kunstwerken« (Brosch 13).[7] Contrary to the stereoscope, however, the particular conjunction of the various and quite diverse references to visual representation in »The Real Thing« will not congeal into one coherent ›picture‹ or idea of visuality and representation in the story but remain contradictory, insoluble, heterogeneous, or, in the words of Whitsitt, »differing within the same« (Whitsitt 306).[8]

II. Cognitive Confusions: (Mis)Perception in »The Real Thing«

One of the most basic and important precepts in cognitive psychology maintains that our previous experiences and the meaning and memories we attach to them, shape how and what we perceive. If we extrapolate from this hypothesis, one could say, simplifying somewhat, that we perceive with our past and our memories of it. Inversely, we also remember depending on what we experience, as new experiences alter our memories. In Frederic Bartlett's phrasing, we bring our »attitude« to what we experience.[9] Since we tend to remember the meaning/significance of what we see rather than the object itself (Anderson 106), one could argue that we structure our seeing according to the influence of past meanings. As we perceive things, we create models of the functioning of this world. As Lakoff points out, there is »nothing more basic than categorization to our thought, perception, action, and speech« (5). We may experience sense perception,

---

7   »We create spatial/pictorial structures in comprehending linguistic pieces of art, and we create linguistic contexts during the successive apprehension of pictorial pieces of art;« *author's translation.*

8   In the background of my argument and indeed my entire essay there lurks an ongoing debate I am intentionally eschewing: do we as humans and readers read and make sense of fictional characters much like, or exactly as, we do of humans, or are fictional characters something apart and ergo exceptional (thus the branding »exceptionality thesis«)? While I find the question per se intriguing, the debate is, upon closer look, not much of a debate. The claims on both sides of the debate are controversial only in their strong versions (fictional characters are exactly/not at all like humans, with the attending consequences for how we make sense of them), which however are easily dismantled; the weak version of the debate (being fictions of the human mind, fictional characters, while ontologically distinct, are inevitably similar to humans and we use similar techniques/scripts etc. for making sense of them), in turn, is not much of a debate. For a little older but still succinct outline of the relation between cognitive science and narratology, see Marie-Laure Ryan's essay in *Style* from 2010.

9   As CT scans of the brain suggest, remembering experiences activates the same regions of the brain that are active while we are making these experiences. Without additional complex data input, the brain could not distinguish between the memory of an experience and the experience itself.

but these sensations are aligned with our percepts, which in turn are the result of idealized cognitive models (ICMs) and provisional heuristics for effectively moving about in the world (Lakoff 68ff; Bierhoff 262ff), such as the availability heuristic, the representativeness heuristic and over-attribution, which more precisely describe processes of selection, projection and generalization. As we acquire new information, we adapt and shift our percepts (Anderson 4ff; 23ff).[10]

As I will show below in more detail, the narrator in James's short story most frequently relies on 1) availability, 2) representativeness, and 3) over-attribution. The availability heuristic (1) focuses on specific, easily accessible and colorful information (Bierhoff 262ff) – such as strong first impression of »types«. When humans filter information through this heuristic, they may assume a false consensus (assuming general agreement to one's judgment or perspective by the majority), commit egocentric errors (overestimating one's own contribution to an interaction because self-information is better stored than partner-information), or work with preemptive hypotheses and/or assimilation (we seek support for what we already believe; we tend to keep false hypotheses and view everything else with the intent to support initial hypotheses; the initial information shapes all successive information, even if incongruous; Bierhoff 287). The representativeness heuristic (2) fosters inductive judgments from atypical cases (e.g. assuming outgroup homogeneity; Bierhoff 266), i.e., that the members of another group are more homogeneous than the members of one's own group. Lastly, over-attribution (3) emphasizes personal characteristics over situational determinants (Bierhoff 267) so that one judges capabilities and effort rather than difficulty and chance (Bierhoff 302).

The defining characteristic of these heuristics is that they afford effectiveness, which means that they tend to unify disparate sensations. Nevertheless, any perception may also instigate multiple percepts or none: if what we see cannot be aligned with our established percepts and previous experience, we may not perceive it at all. In this case, wherever we are faced with »domains of experience that do not have a preconceptual structure of their own« (Lakoff 303), we comprehend experience by importing metaphors from other realms of experience:

> [T]hose concepts which are not directly grounded in experience employ metaphor, metonymy, and mental imagery—all of which go beyond the literal mirroring, or representation, of external reality. [...] The imaginative capacity is also embodied –indirectly– since the metaphors, metonymies and images are based on experience, often bodily experience. [...] [E]very time we categorize something in a way that does not mirror nature, we are using general human imaginative capacities. (Lakoff xiv)

---

10   For an extensive overview of heuristics and decision-making theory, see Betsch, Funke, and Plessner's standard monograph (2011).

For whatever is new and unfamiliar to us, we have to invent or import categories. Some are more adequate than others, and all of them are in need of revision once we attain more experience. If we apply these cognitive models to »The Real Thing«, we can shed light on the narrator's cognitive misapprehensions and on the story as a prototypical exemplification of the unreliability and pitfalls of human cognition.

Perhaps the most notorious example of the narrator's misperceptions is his early claim upon seeing the Monarchs for the first time that »in the pictorial sense« he has »immediately *seen* them« and »seized their type«, thus working in fact with the representativeness heuristic. Numerous similar statements follow in which he purports to »see« them, where »see« could semantically be replaced by »imagine« or »envision.« Crucially, however, the claims to visual perception (see) are seldom attenuated by a semantic shift to imaginative capacity (envision). The ontic factuality of what is allegedly seen, implied by the declarative »see,« culminates in his statement that he is »sure of everything that concern[s] them« (235). Similarly, his rather extreme extension of the representativeness heuristic (seizing their type without knowing their type) belies the neglect of relevant base rates.[11] It appears that the autodiegetic narrator aspires to the panopticism and absolute epistemological authority of the authorial narrators prevalent in much 19th-century realist and naturalist fiction: »It is the elision of these discrete stages of perceiving, representing, and recognizing the world of objects that marks the Cartesian spectator's transcendent, universal view« (Jacobs 48). What Jacobs writes of the narrator in James's *The Sacred Fount*[12] can be applied to the narrator of »The Real Thing«. By eliding the difference between subjective and objective reality, he is not only unreliable but discredits »the posture of detached observation itself« (Jacobs 54). Admittedly, there are repeated epistemological inflections when the narrator concedes that he cannot »of course see the thing in detail« (233) or finds it »odd how quickly [he is] sure of everything that concern[s] them« (235). Nevertheless, the narrator's admonitions that his vision is faulty hardly balance his panopticism in the bulk of the story.

It is ironic that much criticism neglects these admonitions and tends to elide the »discrete stages of perceiving, representing, and recognizing the world of objects« when the story in fact contains a variety of modes of perception (how he sees) and visual codes and media (what he sees): the narrator sees, looks, glances (229), seizes (231), pictures (231), envisions (233), appraises (233), fancies (235), imagines (236), evokes (236), catches and keeps (257). The semantic variety is immense. If one replaces

---

11 The relevant base rate fallacy describes probability judgments that are based on irrelevant information.

12 Written roughly ten years later, this novel may be seen as a continuation of the issues in »The Real Thing«.

the words look and see with synonyms and examines their connotations, they will vary from
- cursory perception (glance),
- references to attire and posture (»she looked too distinguished«),
- experience (»I had seen people painfully reluctant«),
- imagination (retrospective – »I could see the sunny drawing-rooms [...] in which Mrs. Monarch had continuously sat« – and prospective – »I had a vision of the promptitude with which they would launch a table d'hôte«),
- aspiration/expectation (»I looked to a different branch of art«),
- appearance (as an emphasis on the difference between ontology – what is – and epistemology – what we may know or, in this case, see of it),
- to apperception of ontic factuality (passive – see – and active – look at),
- as well as allusions to perceptive distortion (blurred, swam).

Cognition is overwhelmingly visual in the story, to the degree that even non-visual modes of experience and cognition are expressed in visual terms, a tendency which is in keeping with Renate Brosch's claim that in the course of his literary career James increasingly described cognitive processes of his figures as acts of seeing (6) – which in English (Ah, I see) doubles as an expression for comprehension. This in turn does not contribute to cognitive coherence but adversely, due to the story displaying a »diminished faith [...] regarding the capacity of vision to deliver reliable knowledge« (Jacobs 3), creates even more ambiguity.[13]

Moreover, visual cognition is filtered through a variety of modes, while other modes of cognition are neglected, specifically language: »Language, the main nonvisual source of information, is simply done away with as a source of knowledge« (Ludwig 172). When the narrator first meets the Monarchs, he may *see* them all at once but he entirely ›misreads‹ their intention through egocentric error, a misunderstanding amplified by the presence of ›wrong words‹ (»We should like to make it pay«) and the absence of the ones necessary to clear up the misunderstanding. This is, once again, highly ironic because as readers we have access to the story through language only, the semiotic code most ignored in a story of visual cognition. The narrator's misjudgments result from his endeavors to heuristically reduce the complexity of this co-simultaneity of visual modes in order to assimilate complex and plethoric information into his familiar meaning-making frame. This is exacerbated by the various visual codes and media, among them landscape painting (230), portraits (229), black and white illustrations (231), woodcuts (237), portrait photographs (243), advertising photographs

---

13   The narrator's description of the Major's size offers a concise intratextual comment on this heterogeneity, as Ludwig remarks: »the surplus registered is not larger than life but, inversely, larger than the monologic perspectivism [...]. He or she cannot be contained in an imposed perspective« (173).

(233), copies of photographs (243), sketches (231), pictures with and without figures (232), pictures of love (257), of social life (233), etc. To complicate things, these numerous different visual media and genres are repeatedly conflated within one sentence.

In view of such a variety of visual stimuli, the narrator's cognitive confusions and misapprehensions appear as predictable as his attempts to »impose univocal order and sense« (Esch and Warren xi). Looking at the narrator's assertions about things in his field of vision and cognition, we will find that what he relies on is heuristic availability in his initial and subsequent encounters with the Monarchs, i.e., he does not further seek information beyond what he initially sees and, aggravatingly, assumes. As Ludwig puts it: »When Miss Churm poses as a Russian princess, he paints neither his model nor any Russian princess he knows (we may safely assume that he has never met one); rather he produces the representation of something invented.« (171) He relies, thus, on his almost non-existent knowledge about ›their‹ class and reduces their entire personality to effects of that class, assuming outgroup homogeneity, and in addition he over-attributes personal characteristics over situational determinants:

> I could see she had been photographed often, but somehow the very habit that made her good for that purpose unfitted her for mine. [...] But after a few times I began to find her too insurmountably stiff; do what I would with it my drawing looked like a photograph or a copy of a photograph. (243; emphasis mine)

If they fail him as models, it is because of who they are; their desperation, effort and humility, but most importantly the external causes of their plight are given scant mention and appreciation only fleetingly, and mostly toward the end (another egocentric error). In fact, his unreflected and preemptive reliance on these heuristics appears to play a key role in his abilities as an artist:

> the value of such a model as Miss Churm resided precisely in the fact that *she had no positive stamp*, combined of course with the other fact that what she did have was a curious and inexplicable talent for imitation. (245; emphasis mine)

Paradoxically, he appreciates Miss Churm having »no positive stamp« for the power this gives him in attributing whatever content he deems suitable for her representation in his pictures: ›seeing all‹ where there is in fact a cognitive blank prevents the ›adequate‹ representation of the Monarchs but is the prerequisite for the representation of Miss Churm. In both cases, an absence is constitutive for his cognition and artistic ability, but while he is able to fill that blank imaginatively in the case of Miss Churm, his filling of the blank in the case of the Monarchs preempts any further imaginative work. As Miss Churm appears to carry just as much, if not more, specific ›personality‹ as the Monarchs in terms of cultural and educational background, language, attire, habits, there seems to be no logical reason why her person should be more easily rendered than the Monarch's, apart from her unspecified »talent for imitation.« In moral vocabulary, the narrator does not really care about anyone, neither the Monarchs nor Miss Churm, over and beyond how they may serve him and his ambitions. Over the course of the story, he gets to know the Monarchs a little better (he already knows Muss Churm, if one can talk about »knowing« at all) and has sufficient opportunities to revise his judgments, to get to know »their types« (and here I mean all of his models), to appreciate them and their situation, but he makes no use of these opportunities – in fact, it would seem that in the case of the Monarchs, these opportunities rather are nuisances to him.

The narrator's probably most obvious reduction relies on preemptive hypotheses and assimilation. All judgments subsequent to his initial impression of the Monarchs are made and shaped in accordance with that impression. He may not yet be prescient about the impending predicament which they more or less haplessly instigate – or in other words: the second rate trick into which they get him–, but this is not because he alters his initial assessment; rather he fails to comprehend the potential consequences of that assessment. As Phyllis van Slyck points out, James's story challenges the illusion that »one understands what one sees« (217). While all humans are potentially subject to this illusion, it is how we deal with it that makes the illusion an ethical issue; the narrator in »The Real Thing« never really confronts the truth of »his (or her) subjective shaping of reality« (218), which makes his excusable cognitive »failure« simultaneously a significantly less excusable moral failure. In unsympathetic terms, we could call him self-absorbed, egoistic, superficial, vain, and arrogant.

Pointing out that the narrator is unreliable in the literary sense thus does not quite do justice to the complexity of the story if this unreliability is merely premised in his self-revealing comments. The narrator is unreliable not simply because he misjudges but because he is cognitively overtaxed, respectively unwilling to adequately deal with cognitive complexity, and thus no more or less unreliable than any human being under certain circumstances might be. If we judge his judgments, we enter the realm of morality and ethics, and here it is not so much the Monarchs but the narrator who fails, not because his misjudgments would be completely avoidable, but because he fails, in the framework of Hans-Georg Gadamer's hermeneutic circle, to revise, reflect and adapt his prejudices (see also Armstrong 2019, 139-141). Selection, projection and generalization are filters we all employ, indeed have to employ, if we want to maintain some degree of agency, moral and otherwise, but they need to be paired with self-reflexivity and self-awareness:[14] »the establishment of habitual modes of pattern-

---

[14] In an essay on what readers may learn from the experiences of fictional characters, Michael Butter makes a similar point (albeit within an overall different context and to a different end): »Die Herstellung dieses Zusammenhangs [between complex and ambivalent signs and our

formation is both a blessing and a curse« (Armstrong summarizing William James, 2019, 142) because it enables fast coping, reaction, and learning, but it also makes us »vulnerable to the danger of becoming locked in behaviors« (142).

Neither, then, should it be a surprise that the narrator's heuristic reduction of complexity leads to misjudgments nor that critical readings in their exegesis tend to replicate the reduction of cognitive complexity, because it is a necessary and inevitable cognitive human process. The decisive –ethical– difference lies in the degree of awareness and self-reflexivity we bring to that reduction and in our willingness to question ourselves and our judgments. The ›deviousness‹ or propensity of the story to encourage these reductions is grounded in its engendering of ambiguity, its tendency to defy and resist disambiguation and the imposition of »univocal order and sense.« In psychological terminology this amounts to the inability of coming to a judgment and the multiple coexistence of contradictory assessments (in one person) called cognitive dissonance. Put into the cultural historical context, this seems fitting, because it goes hand in hand with what one might call visual dissonance.

III. Crisis of Seeing, Crisis of Cognition: Historical Context

Granted, one can appreciate the complexity, the phenomenological ruminations, and the stylistic mastery of »The Real Thing« without knowing too much about the cultural historical context. However, one would miss the many subtle allusions to late 19th century »visual culture« that James has clearly built into the story (and that are part of many other stories and novels by James). More importantly, one would be left with a truncated understanding of the facets and layers of the story – without being aware of it.

The various different kinds of media and visual representations depicted and/or alluded to in the story constitute an indirect reference to visual media in the second half of the 19th century in general and to the medium of photography in particular. Given that ›photography‹ comes in a variety of different media and genres, one has to differentiate among a variety of visual codes and genres. At the time James published »The Real Thing«, the daguerreotype was almost extinct, although occasionally re-photographed onto calo- or ferrotypes or onto paper-based film in order to salvage it from disappearance. But ambrotypes and ferrotypes were still in use alongside Disdéri's popular carte-de-visites (whose pervasiveness is likely to have caused James's disap-

---

efforts to make sense of them] erfordert beträchtlichen kognitiven Aufwand – und das Vermeiden von interpretatorischen Schnellschüssen. Einen solchen leistet sich aber der Erzähler […].« (313) According to Butter, the narrator's most dramatic shortcoming is his inability/unwillingness to reflect upon his mistaken assumptions.

proval in contrast to his early appreciation of the daguerreotype) and the even more popular Kodak camera patented by Eastman in 1888.

In addition, visual capacities were tested by tableaux vivants, panoramas, stereoscopes, dioramas, early animation devices such as phenakistoscopes, zoetropes, etc.[15] The complexity of visual decoding was enhanced by the different genres in which visual media found expression, such as advertising pictures, photojournalism, post mortem pictures, medallions, photographic pairs in books en face (which demanded dialogic apprehension and occasionally developed a narrative dimension), and hand colored pictures (which subverted the gap between representation and surface). Audience accounts of the popular visual spectacles give witness to a curious mixture of the ›natural‹ and the sensational: the habitually inured distinction between real and unreal was disrupted just because the illusions were so effectual that they amounted to a kind of naturalistic sensationalism.[16]

All this is important for the story because, as Jonathan Crary shows, the »new empirical knowledge of vision and techniques of the visible« (5) that developed in the 19th century go hand in hand with, or rather entail, a »new kind of observer« (5). As he points out, »there is a tendency to conflate all optical devices in the nineteenth century as equally implicated in a vague collective drive to higher and higher standards of verisimilitude« (16); if that was the case, there would have been no need for a new kind of observer, or a new kind of science, for that matter. However, as Crary continues, such »teleological approaches most often neglect entirely how these devices were expressions of nonveridical models of perception« (17). By this he means that in many devices, what is seen is not really »there« but constructed in the human brain. It is, in other words, phantasmagoric, as in a Wheatstone stereoscope, for example. In other words, and more generally, »[v]ision is literally hermeneutic–a circular, recursive process of assembling parts into wholes« (Armstrong 2018, 139).

Criticism of James and »The Real Thing«, however, tends to focus on photography only, probably because of James's many remarks about it. Regarding the technological aspects of photography, which affected the evaluation of its aesthetic merit, the actual mechanics of photography effectively contributed to the proliferation of visual codes and their decoding. In focusing on James's disdainful remarks on photography in his reviews and prefaces as well as on the narrator's equally disparaging comments, critics

---

15 Some panoramas even had live animals placed in them, accompanying music and sounds, as well as wind. They were, contrary to the critical focus on their unsettling of the real through visual illusion, anticipating the cinematic, aimed at »deceiving« all senses. In his essay »Techniques of the Observer« (1988), Jonathan Crary provides a comprehensive and detailed discussion of the development of visuality (in science, philosophy, art, and entertainment) in the 19th century.

16 Anno Mungen provides an excellent collection of documents (from announcements, programs and reviews to essays and miscellanies) regarding panoramas, tableaux vivants and other forms of visual ›spectacle‹ (2006).

tend to demonstrate a limited recognition of photography's artistry and modes of production (not uncommon in the years that first witnessed its mass production) that may in part stem from an inability to distinguish ›bad‹ from ›good‹ photography. Understanding photography requires the learning of codes and conventions just as much as understanding painting requires historically and culturally acquired knowledge. Towards the turn of the 19ᵗʰ century »the debate as to the aesthetic character of photography [Slater claims] conventionally rest[ed] on the distinction between scientific and artistic vision, fact and fiction, objectivity and subjectivity« (220), thus the dominant understanding of photography emphasized its mechanics while downplaying its aesthetics.

In contrast, the famous photographer Peter Henry Emerson pointed out as early as 1889 that it is not the machine, but the people using it who choose the picture, so that the camera enforces a transferal, not a loss, of creative control (Michaels 218).[17] Walter Benn Michaels aptly points out that for Emerson »the fact that almost anyone can take a picture is no more damaging to photography than the fact that almost anyone can write is damaging to poetry« (220). Even more importantly, it follows from accepting the conventionality of decoding photographs and other visual modes that the viewer does add something to the picture. It is not pure referent and surface, but rather product and producer of ambiguity. According to Michaels, if one denies »the ambiguity of the photograph, [one] denies also what Berger calls the ›social function of subjectivity,‹ the potential for each viewer of a photograph […] to construct a personal relation with it« (237).

Despite the significance of media and visuality in the story and the attending moment in cultural history, it should not be forgotten that the story is a piece of ekphrasis: there are no visual codes, only their textual, and thus metaphorized and metonymized, rendering. Considering that in a fictional text words are all we have for visualizing (= imagining!) the represented pictures, drawings, illustrations, etc. there are precious few actual descriptions of what is allegedly put on canvas. It is up to the reader to imagine what we might see, or what the narrator is seeing. In that regard, too, the story is phenomenological, on yet another level.

We might leave it at that, were it not for the confounding and at the same time illuminating fact that much criticism of the story repeats the filtering and disambiguation by the narrator (both the experiencing and the experienced I). To avoid misunderstandings: the purpose of the next section is not to depreciate critics and their attempts to analyze and interpret the story, much less to suggest that akin to the narrator's disambiguation, there is an ethical dimension to this critical disambiguation. After all, critics do not depreciate people in writing about »The Real Thing«. What I aim

---

17   This view gained prevalence only two decades later with the ascendance of other famous photographers such as Stieglitz, Coburn, or Steichen.

to show is that the story is not only *about* impressions, cognition, and phenomenology, but also *engenders* – verifiably – typical phenomenological processes in readers.

IV. Critical Reductions of »The Real Thing«

The story is among the most analyzed pieces of James' short fiction. Independent of one's critical view as to what end the story actually does what it does, »The Real Thing« is a complex comment on reality, representation, fiction, and art – phenomenological fiction, as Armstrong calls it. The many plausible and sustained critical readings given to it are probably the best indication of its ambiguity and cognitive equivocation, despite or perhaps because of its apparent closure. However, a significant amount of criticism tends to take its task of disambiguation somewhat too seriously, testifying to a »tendency to impose univocal order and sense on language that strongly resists such acts of force« (Esch & Warren xi). Critical disambiguation focusing on reality, representation and cognition in »The Real Thing« works with one or more of the following reductions:

(1) Exteriority: Based on the fact that Henry James's reviews, prefaces, notebooks, other critical commentaries as well as his autobiography brim with remarks on fiction and representation, art and photography as well as with painting, drawing and theater metaphors, it is assumed that this predilection is reflected in »The Real Thing« (Schwarzschild; Grossman).[18]

(2) Thematic focus / correlation: As part of the critical work, the focus has to be narrowed to what seem the most pertinent comments, which often amounts to a reduction of focus on one medium, namely photography. Biographical fallacy creates a correlative relationship between what James says about representation, art and photography outside the story and what the narrator says about it inside the story (Nadel; Higgins).[19]

(3) Ontological distinction: By equating James with the narrator – mostly asymmetrically, i.e. they are not identical but rather the narrator represents James's views –, the story is incorporated into the textual universe of all that James has written.

---

18 For example, in a 1859 review on the character of Carter in De Forest's *Miss Ravenel's Conversion* James writes that Carter is »daguerreotyped from nature« (491), other frequently cited examples are found in the prefaces to *The Golden Bowl* (1904), *The Sacred Fount* (1901), or *The Portrait of a Lady* (1881). In his fiction he has written about a host of diverse painters and artists (listed in Tintner) in addition to his fictional ones; and in his autobiography he comments on his picture being taken as a boy: »Beautiful most decidedly the lost art of the daguerreotype« (52) and on the fact that he has kept that picture all his life.

19 The same is true for James's comments on the Monarchs: in his notebooks, he calls them »clean and stiff and stupid« (103).

Therefore, what James has written about photography, for example, can be treated not as a mere intertext but as integral to the story (Sonstegard; Schwarzschild; Nadel).

(4) Argumentative heterogeneity: At this point, critical ventures branch out into three lines of argument. Among the most frequent disambiguations (Tick; Grossman) are those that argue »that James's story identifies the real thing with photography, a medium he supposedly despised« (Burrows 256), turning the story into a »straight-forward parable about James's supposed scorn for the real thing« and, by extension, photography (Burrows 256).[20] Unsurprisingly, another critical route is to claim the opposite, namely that James, whether he openly admitted it or not, was fascinated with photography, appropriated its »pictorial sense« (Higgins 662) or saw in it, for his New York Edition, a means of attracting a larger audience, making it more marketable but also adding something aesthetic to it (Sonstegard; Schwarzschild; Nadel). The third critical disambiguation focuses on those remarks by James in and outside the story that attest to his ambivalence about photography (Grossman; Miller).

Cognitive psychology understands heuristics as reductions of complexity necessary and inevitable in order to effectively arrive at judgments and in order to be able to act at all at reasonable speeds. Therefore, the above comments are not meant to discredit or stereotype the extant criticism on the whole. Rather, they aim to emphasize how readings of the story replicate the mechanisms of cognitive heuristics and their potential for misjudgments and stereotypes described in the story, as well as the attempts to alleviate the resulting ambiguity in evaluating and interpreting the story.

Generally, James's commentary in various genres changes over time and is repeatedly contradictory, so that »[a]ttempts in the direction of totalizing Henry James's reactions to photography [and various other visual media; my insertion], even if the narrative involves a sensitive tracing of his shifting views, are unconvincing in that they fail to take account« (Rawlings 459)[21] of James's own ambivalent and contradictory comments as well as of the fact that teller and tale should not be conflated:

---

20   Crucial to this argument are James's derisive comments in his *Notebooks* on the Monarchs: they »have no pictorial sense. They are only clean and stiff and stupid« (1947: 103). For him they stood for English amateurishness (1987: 55).

21   Rawlings completes the sentence with a reference to the »Kodak Moment.« Apart from providing a concise history of the photograph, he is one of the few to address the fact that there was a tremendous difference between the initial daguerreotypes and the later Kodaks, which were mass products and available to a mass of amateur artists, making it radically different from what Alfred Stieglitz and Alvin Langdon Coburn produced. However, he does not fully heed his own advice when ›totalizing‹ Walter Benjamin, who also saw political and revolutionary potential in the loss of aura due to mass production (137).

In fact, James is not ignorant of the need for, and market conditions of, production; he expounds it in »The Madonna of the Future«, and it is, after all, a deluxe edition the narrator of »The Real Thing« illustrates.

Gerade weil James' fiktionale Texte, besonders die späteren, eine skeptisch-relativis-
tische Position zur Wahrnehmung beziehen und den Glauben an die Präzedenz ›un-
schuldiger‹ Sinneswahrnehmungen als Illusion enttarnen, ist eine Übernahme seiner
theoretischen Positionen der Übertragung lebensweltlicher Wahrnehmung auf die
Textproduktion und Rezeption nicht möglich. (Brosch 7)[22]

In effect, the homogenization of James's shifting views in both literary and non-literary
texts amounts to what Lakoff identifies as typical of human cognition: prototyping, i.e.
the graded categorization that ranks one member of a set/category as more central than
another.

   Even if we abide by the latter admonition and neglect or at least carefully differentiate the heterogeneity of James's comments on art and representation outside the
story, we are still faced with an abundance of heterogeneous kinds of representation,
media and visual codes inside the story, as well as insoluble contradictory observations
by the narrator regarding these ›visualities.‹ The stereotyping of »The Real Thing«
thus appears to replicate the heuristic reduction of complexity and cognitive proliferation by the narrator in the story.

V. Conclusion

We should pay attention to, but not take at face-value what Henry James has written.
The explicitness of some of his statements regarding »The Real Thing« as well as
diverse visual media and modes of representation belies their inconsistency with many
of his other statements regarding similar matters and the complexity of the story itself.
»The Real Thing« might, in fact, be telling us that there is no real thing; that there is
only »empty chatter« (Vieilledent 34). Nor is the story, contrary to Vieilledent (34), an
allegory about writing producing the real thing. The proliferation of modes and codes of
perception and the subsequent cognitive ambiguity argued for in this essay would
preempt such a reading. Rather, as Ludwig argues, the story is experiential, interac-
tional, and dramatic (174); or in the phrasing of John Armstrong, the story is a drama of
impressions (1983). Granted, many nineteenth-century writers of fiction wanted their
texts understood not as written but as visual and corporeal artifacts (Flannery 5). But
while readers can of course transpose the textual semiotic code into other codes or
simply metaphorize it, the story itself cannot. What »The Real Thing« offers is a

---

22   It is *because* James's fictional texts, especially the later ones, assume a skeptical-relativistic stance
     towards perception and disclose the belief in the precedence of ›innocent‹ sensory perception as
     an illusion that it is not possible to adopt his theoretical positions regarding the transferal of
     worldly perception onto text production and reception. *Author's translation and emphasis*

brilliant textual, semantic transposition of real visual, historical and corporeal phenomena current not only at the end of the 19th century, but characteristic of the human cognition. But the story does not stop there. Neuroscience can help shed light on how cognition presumably »works« in the human brain, but »it cannot tell us what to do, morally« (Armstrong 2018, 146). »The Real Thing« – fortunately, I might add – does not do that either, but it does something better: it shows us and tells us about the ethical and moral consequences of unreflected cognition and hasty judgment, and it engages, almost forces us as readers to reflect upon that ethical dimension. To the end, the narrator does not fully understand the lesson so that we as readers may.

Works Cited

Anderson, John R. (2009): *Cognitive Psychology and Its Implications.* 7th Ed. New York: Palgrave Macmillan.

Armstrong, John (2018): »Henry James and Neuroscience: Cognitive Universals and Cultural Differences.« In: *The Henry James Review* 39, 133-151.

Armstrong, John (1983): *The Phenomenology of Henry James.* Chapel Hill and London: The University of North Carolina Press.

Benjamin, Walter (1977): *Illuminationen.* Frankfurt a.M.: Suhrkamp.

Betsch, Tilmann/Funke, Joachim/Plessner, Henning (2011): *Denken – Urteilen, Entscheiden, Problemlösen.* Berlin and Heidelberg, Springer.

Bierhoff, Hans-Werner (2006): *Sozialpsychologie.* 6th Ed. Stuttgart: W. Kohlhammer.

Brosch, Renate (2000): *Krisen des Sehens.* Tübingen: Stauffenburg.

Burrows, Stuart (2002): »Stereotyping Henry James.« In: *The Henry James Review* 23, 255-264.

Butter, Michael (2012): »Was Leser mit Figuren lernen: Henry James' ›The Real Thing‹ and Stephen Cranes ›An Experiment in Misery‹.« In: Pape, Lilith/Krämer, Olav/Lampert, Fabian (Eds.): *Figurenwissen.* Berlin: de Gruyter, 307-323.

Crary, Joanathan (1988): »Techniques of the Observer.« In: *October* 45, 3-35.

Esch, Deborah/Warren, Jonathan (1999): Preface to the Second Edition. *The Turn of the Screw.* By Henry James. New York & London: Norton. xi-xiii.

Flannery, Denis (2000): *Henry James: A Certain Illusion.* Aldershot: Ashgate.

Grossman, Julie (1994): »›It's the Real Thing‹: Henry James, Photography, and *The Golden Bowl.*« In: *The Henry James Review* 15, 309-328.

Higgins, Charles (1982): »Photographic Aperture: Coburn's Frontispieces to James's New York Edition.« In: *American Literature* 53:4, 661-675.

Iuliano, Fiorenzo (2019): »Making and Unmaking (Im)Possible Worlds: Language Games, Naming, and Necessities in ›The Real Thing‹.« In: *The Henry James Review* 40, 137-154.

Jacobs, Karen (2001): *The Eye's Mind.* Ithaca and London: Cornell UP.

James, Henry (1879/1963): »The Madonna of the Future.« *The Complete Tales of Henry James.* Ed. Leon Edel. Vol. 3. London: Rupert Hart-Davis.

– (1892/1963). »The Real Thing.« *The Complete Tales of Henry James.* Ed. Leon Edel. Vol. 8. London: Rupert Hart-Davis.

– (1867). »Miss Ravenel's Conversion.« In: *Nation* 4: 491-492.

– (1913-1917/1956): *Henry James: Autobiography*. Ed. F.W. Dupee. London: W.H. Allen.

– (1987): *The Complete Notebooks of Henry James*. Ed. Leon Edel and Lyall H. Powers. New York: Oxford UP.

– (1947): *The Notebooks of Henry James*. Ed. F.O. Matthiessen and Kenneth B. Murdock. New York: Oxford UP.

James, William (1890/1950): *The Principles of Psychology*. New York: Dover.

Lakoff, George (1987): *Women, Fire, and Dangerous Things*. Chicago and London: University of Chicago Press.

Ludwig, Sämi (2002): *Pragmatist Realism: The Cognitive Paradigm in American Realist Texts*. Madison: The University of Wisconsin Press.

Michaels, Walter Benn (1987): *The Gold Standard and the Logic of Naturalism*. Berkeley etc.: University of California Press.

Miller, J. Hillis (1995): »The ›Grafted‹ Image: James on Illustration.« In: McWhirter, David (Ed.): *Henry James's New York Edition*. Stanford: Stanford UP, 138-141.

Mitchell, W.J.T. (1994): *Picture Theory*. Chicago and London: The University of Chicago Press.

Mungen, Anno (2006): *BilderMusik: Panoramen, tableaux vivants und Lichtbilder als multimediale Darstellungsformen in Theater- und Musikaufführungen vom 19. bis zum frühen 20. Jahrhundert*. 2 Vols. Remscheid: Gardez!.

Nadel, Ira B (1995): »Visual Culture: The Photo Frontispieces to the New York Edition.« In: McWhirter, David (Ed.): *Henry James's New York Edition*. Stanford: Stanford UP, 90-108.

Rawlings, Peter (1998): »A Kodak Refraction of Henry James's ›The Real Thing‹.« In: *Journal of American Studies* 32:3, 447-462.

Ryan, Marie-Laure (2010): »Narratology and Cognitive Science: A Problematic Relation.« In: *Style* 44:4, 469-495.

Schwarzschild, Edward L. (1996): »Revising Vulnerability: Henry James's Confrontation with Photography.« In: *Texas Studies in Literature and Language* 38:1, 51-78.

Slater, Don (1995): »Photography and Modern Vision: The Spectacle of ›Natural Magic‹.« In: Jenks, Chris (Ed.): *Visual Culture*. London and New York: Routledge, 218-237.

Sonstegard, Adam (2003): »Painting, Photography, and Fidelity in *The Tragic Muse*.« In: *The Henry James Review* 24, 27-44.

Tick, Stanley (1993): »Positives and Negatives: Henry James vs. Photography.« In: *Nineteenth Century Studies* 7, 69-101.

Tintner, Adeline R. (1993): *Henry James and the Lust of the Eyes*. Baton Rouge and London: Louisiana State UP.

van Slyck, Phyllis (2001): »Trapping the Gaze: Objects of Desire in James's Early and Late Fiction.« In: Dewey, Joseph/Horvath, Brooke (Eds.): ›*The Finer Thread, The Tighter Weave*‹: *Essays on the Short Fiction of Henry James*. West Lafayette: Purdue UP, 217-234.

Vieilledent, Catherine (1984): »Representation and Reproduction: A Reading of Henry James's ›The Real Thing‹.« In: Royot, Daniel (Ed.): *Interface: Essays on History, Myth and Art in American Literature*. Montpellier: Université Paul Valery, 31-49.

Whitsitt, Sam (1995): »A Lesson in Reading: Henry James's ›The Real Thing‹.« In: *The Henry James Review* 16, 304-314.

Bernhard Stricker

Rezension zu: Grandl, Matthias/Möller, Melanie (Hg.) (2021): Wissen *en miniature*. Theorie und Epistemologie der Anekdote

Wiesbaden: Harrassowitz Verlag (= Episteme in Bewegung. Beiträge zu einer transdisziplinären Wissensgeschichte, hrsg. von Gyburg Uhlmann im Auftrag des Sonderforschungsbereichs 980 »Episteme in Bewegung. Wissenstransfer von der Alten Welt bis in die Frühe Neuzeit«, Band 19), 316 S., ISBN 978-3-447-11540-7

Anekdotische Evidenz genießt keinen guten Ruf. Wo sie im öffentlichen oder politischen Diskurs beschworen wird, geschieht das in aller Regel zum Zweck der Diskreditierung der von anderen erhobenen Wissensansprüche, deren Bezeichnung als ›anekdotische Evidenz‹ impliziert, es würden aus einem wenig belastbaren Einzelfall ungedeckte Schlüsse gezogen. Nicht immer aber galt die Anekdote wegen ihrer Fokussierung auf den Einzelfall schon als epistemisch unzuverlässig. Dass sie am Maßstab heutiger empirischer, etwa statistischer Methoden gemessen unwissenschaftlich erscheinen mag, sollte nicht übersehen lassen, dass die Anekdote den Status eines »zentralen Transfermediums antiken Wissens« (S. 3) beanspruchen kann. So lautet die programmatische Feststellung der Herausgeber*innen Matthias Grandl und Melanie Möller in der Einleitung zu einem Band, der sich unter dem Titel *Wissen* en miniature. *Theorie und Epistemologie der Anekdote* dem epistemischen Potential dieser kurzen Textform widmet und der dabei nicht nur einen Bogen von der Antike bis in die Moderne spannt, sondern neben Texten auch Bilder mit in den Blick nimmt. Mit einem historisch und disziplinär breit gefächerten Spektrum von Phänomenen und Zugangsweisen gelingt es dem Band auf knapp 300 Seiten hervorragend, die Anekdote als Wissensform zu profilieren.

Dass die Aufsätze dabei auch in ihrer Gesamtheit nur exemplarischen Charakter in Bezug auf ein so weit gefasstes Phänomen wie anekdotisches Wissen beanspruchen können, entspricht durchaus dem Gegenstand der Anekdote. Deren besondere Eignung, den Ereignischarakter von Geschichte gerade durch die Unterbrechung kontinuierlicher und teleologischer Narrative hervorzukehren, war bereits von Walter Benjamin entdeckt worden, bevor die Anekdote in den Arbeiten namhafter Vertreter des *New Historicism* wie Stephen Greenblatt und Joel Fineman (Greenblatt 1988; Fineman 1989) eine bis heute andauernde Aufwertung erfuhr. Mit ihrem dezidiert epistemischen Anekdotenbegriff verorten sich die Herausgeber*innen des vorliegen-

den Bandes klar in dieser kulturwissenschaftlichen Denktradition und grenzen sich
von stärker literaturhistorischen, gattungspoetologischen oder narratologischen An-
sätzen ab, wie sie etwa der jüngst von Christian Moser und Reinhard M. Möller her-
ausgegebene Band *Anekdotisches Erzählen. Zur Geschichte und Poetik einer kleinen Form*
(De Gruyter, 2022) repräsentiert.

Mit der ›kleinen Form‹ ist ein aktuelles literatur- und kulturwissenschaftliches
Forschungsfeld benannt, in dessen Rahmen anekdotische Textformen neben anderen
Gattungen der Kurzprosa seit einiger Zeit wieder eine gesteigerte Aufmerksamkeit
erfahren (Fleming 2011; Fleming 2012; Gilly 2018). Hat der Begriff der ›kleinen Form‹
seinen Ursprung in der Untersuchung von Textgenres, wie sie sich seit dem 19. Jahrhundert zunächst im Zeitungsfeuilleton etabliert haben, so liegt der Fokus bei den
Altphilolog*innen Matthias Grandl und Melanie Möller entsprechend ihrer Verortung
im Kontext des Sonderforschungsbereichs 980 »Episteme in Bewegung. Wissenstransfer von der Alten Welt bis in die Frühe Neuzeit« (FU Berlin) eher auf der Vor-
moderne. Obwohl es dem Band ausgezeichnet gelingt, eine Brücke von der Antike über
die Frühe Neuzeit bis zur Moderne zu schlagen, fällt auf, dass die für das Forschungsfeld
der kleinen Form so eminent wichtige erste Hälfte des 20. Jahrhunderts mit keinem
Beitrag repräsentiert ist. Die solcherart klaffende Lücke wird hingegen durch die
Vielzahl von Querverbindungen, die sich für aufmerksame Leser*innen des Bandes
zwischen den einzelnen Beiträge ergeben, kompensiert.

Der Band versammelt Ergebnisse des von Melanie Möller in der zweiten Förderphase
des SFB 980 (2016-2020) geleiteten Teilprojekts »Die Anekdote als Medium des Wis-
senstransfers«. Die philosophischen und philologischen, kunstgeschichtlichen und
komparatistischen Beiträge gehen auf eine im Rahmen dieses Projekts im Oktober 2018
veranstaltete Tagung zurück. Die Anordnung der Beiträge in vier Sektionen folgt einer
primär thematischen Gruppierung, bildet aber zugleich eine annähernd chronologische
Reihenfolge. Der erste Abschnitt zur »Archäologie der Anekdote« umfasst drei Beiträge mit dem Fokus auf der Antike. Unter der Überschrift »Die Anekdote im Spiegel
europäischer Literaturen« sind anschließend vier Aufsätze versammelt, die einen
Bogen vom 13. bis zum 19. Jahrhundert mit einem klaren Schwerpunkt auf der Frühen
Neuzeit schlagen. Mit »Theorie und Geschichte der Anekdote« sind wiederum drei
Aufsätze überschrieben, die Texte und Autoren vom 17. bis zum 20. Jahrhundert um-
fassen. Den Schluss bilden zwei Artikel zum Verhältnis der Anekdote zu Bildmedien,
deren Sektionstitel »Die Anekdote im Bild« insofern irreführend ist, als dass sich die
Aufsätze mit der Bedeutung von Anekdoten im kunsttheoretischen und kunst-
historischen Diskurs, nicht aber mit anekdotischen Sujets *in* der Malerei befassen.

Vorneweg findet sich ein kurzer Essay von Jürgen Paul Schwindt mit dem Titel
»Was weiß die Anekdote – und wie? Grundlinien einer Theorie der Lücke (nach
Sueton)«, dessen Sonderstellung nicht nur durch den grundlegenden Status der von
ihm adressierten Frage nach dem Charakter anekdotischen Wissens begründet, son-

dern auch durch den Umstand gerechtfertigt erscheint, dass er selbst anekdotische Züge trägt: Schwindt verleiht seinen Überlegungen zur wirkungsgeschichtlichen Bedeutung der biographischen Geschichtsschreibung Suetons eine autobiographische Dimension, indem er die Geschichte seiner eigenen Hinwendung zu dem zunächst vernachlässigten Autor der Kaiserviten erzählt. Dass seine Entdeckung Suetons nicht viel weniger als die Wiederentdeckung der Philologie markiert, mit der Schwindts Name seit geraumer Zeit verbunden ist (vgl. Schwindt 2009), erweist sich dabei als dem Umstand geschuldet, dass – wie Schwindt schreibt – »die Anekdote als literarische Kurzform, darin dem Epigramm nicht unähnlich, geeignet ist, die Erkenntnisweise(n) der Literatur besonders prägnant zur Darstellung zu bringen. Die Anekdote lässt sich gewissermaßen als eine Versuchsanordnung beschreiben, in der das markanteste Moment des gewöhnlichen Experiments außer Kraft gesetzt wird: Die Struktur des ›Immer wenn, dann‹. Die Erkenntnis, die die Anekdote zu Tage fördert, ist nicht verallgemeinerbar.« (S. 35) Eine passendere Vorrede zu diesem Band lässt sich schwer vorstellen.

Die disziplinäre Verortung eines Forschungsprojekts zur Anekdote in der Klassischen Philologie mag zunächst überraschen, denn die Blütezeit dieser Textgattung wird gern auf das 18. Jahrhundert datiert und vor allem in der französischen Literatur gesehen. Dagegen war in der Antike wohl das Phänomen (unter der Bezeichnung des Apophtegmas), nicht aber der Begriff der ›Anekdote‹ geläufig (Schäfer 1982, 11). Dieser geht erst auf den spätantiken Autor Prokop von Caesarea (ca. 500-562) zurück, der neben seiner offiziellen Tätigkeit als Historiograph der Feldzüge des oströmischen Kaisers Justinian I. eine *historia arcana* verfasste, die er wegen ihrer deutlichen Kritik an den Zuständen am kaiserlichen Hof nicht veröffentlichte (gr. *anekdoton* = ›unveröffentlicht‹). Wenn Rüdiger Zill, der sich mit zahlreichen einschlägigen Arbeiten zur Anekdote längst als Experte für dieses Thema etabliert hat (Zill 2014a, 2014b), in seinem Beitrag (»Geschichten in Bewegung. Zum Funktionswandel der Anekdote im 17. und 18. Jahrhundert«) überraschend feststellt, dass Prokops Berichte »paradoxerweise oft keine Anekdoten im starken heutigen Sinne sind« (S. 164), so zeigt sich darin eine Diskrepanz zwischen *res et verba*, Sache und Begriff, die für die ›bewegte Geschichte‹ der Anekdote an zahlreichen Stellen relevant ist. So gelangt Zill, indem er die semantischen und medialen Transferleistungen nachzeichnet, die mit der Einbürgerung des Terminus *anecdote* im Französischen im Laufe des 17. Jahrhunderts einhergingen, zu dem Nachweis, dass Prokop als der Verfasser von ›Geheimgeschichten‹ Vorbildwirkung entfaltet habe, der Begriff der Anekdote sich dabei aber von einem primär formal-publikationstechnischen zu einem inhaltlich bestimmten Konzept gewandelt habe. Die Pointe von Zills Essay könnte man so formulieren: Die Anekdote im heutigen Sinne ist eigentlich nur als Effekt einer Rezeption von Texten und der mit ihnen einhergehenden Umbesetzungen des Begriffs zu verstehen. Eine der Stärken von *Wissen* en miniature. *Theorie und Epistemologie der Anekdote* besteht entsprechend darin, dass der Band

Transferprozesse begriffs- oder kulturgeschichtlicher Art nachvollziehbar werden lässt und so Wissen in der Tat als das Ergebnis von Bewegungen durch Zeiten und Räume hindurch begreifbar macht.

Wenig überraschend fungiert dabei immer wieder Hans Blumenberg als Stich-wortgeber, der mit seiner Studie *Das Lachen der Thrakerin. Eine Urgeschichte der Theorie* (1987) und einer etwa durch seine »Glossen zu Anekdoten« (1983-1988) dokumen-tierten Vorliebe für philosophische Miniatur-Narrative der Anekdotenforschung neue Impulse vermittelt hat. (Und zu dessen Werk Melanie Möller ebenfalls einen sehr lesenswerten Sammelband mit dem Titel *Prometheus gibt nicht auf. Antike Welt und modernes Leben in Hans Blumenbergs Philosophie* (Fink 2015) publiziert hat.) Der Aufsatz von Katharina Hertfelder (»Bewegungslinien der Anekdote bei Hans Blumenberg«) ist ganz explizit Blumenbergs Kommentaren zu dem besonderen Typus der ›Wander-anekdote‹ gewidmet. Zu den zahlreichen Querverbindungen, die sich zwanglos zwi-schen den Aufsätzen in *Wissen en miniature* ergeben, gehört, dass sich die Reihe der von Hertfelder kommentierten »Fallgeschichten« Blumenbergs (zu Thales, Newton und Einstein) durch drei weitere anekdotische ›Fälle‹ ergänzen ließe, die im Zentrum der Beiträge von Melanie Möller (»Am Anfang war… die Kloake. Wissensanekdoten in antiker Biographik«), Mira Becker-Sawatzky (»Anekdoten im frühneuzeitlichen Kunstdiskurs. Kontexte und Funktionen am Beispiel akademischer Zirkel in Rom und Paris«) und Verena Olejniczak Lobsien (»Andrew Marvell, oder die Kunst des Schwebens«) stehen. Möllers Aufsatz skizziert, ausgehend von den Biographien der ersten Philologen in Suetons *Grammatici et rhetores* und damit im Gefolge Jürgen Paul Schwindts, die anekdotisch beglaubigte Genese der Philologie, wobei ihr besonderes Augenmerk dem versehentlichen Sturz des »Urvater[s] römischer Philologie« (S. 72), Krates von Mallos, in die Kanalisation gilt – eine regelrechte ›Parallel-Anekdote‹ (wie man in Anlehnung an Plutarch sagen könnte) zum Fall des Urphilosophen in eine Zisterne. Die bereits auf solcherlei ›Fälle‹ fokussierte Aufmerksamkeit der Leser*innen wird in dem umfangreichen Beitrag von Mira Becker-Sawatzky besonders die Anek-dote über einen spanischen Adligen goutieren, der auf der Reise nach Neapel in eine Gebirgsschlucht stürzt und zum Dank für seine Unversehrtheit ein Votivgemälde in Auftrag gibt, in dem er die Begebenheit wahrheitsgetreu dargestellt haben möchte. Weil sein Fall jedoch zu der vom Bildbetrachter abgewandten Seite hin geschah, lässt er die erste Version des Bildes dahingehend korrigieren, dass er selbst und sein Sturz darin nicht mehr zu sehen sind. Im Mittelpunkt von Verena Olejniczak Lobsiens Aufsatz schließlich steht die Ausdeutung, welcher der englische Dichter Andrew Marvell in seinem Gedicht *The First Anniversary of the Government under his Highness the Lord Protector* (1654/55) den Sturz Oliver Cromwells vom Pferd, der wegen seiner ominös anmutenden Bedeutung seinerzeit heiß diskutiert wurde, unterzieht.

Die Betrachtung der Anekdote als einer Form der literarischen Skepsis wiederum verbindet Lobsiens Artikel mit den Aufsätzen von Simon Godart (»Heiterkeit. Anekdotische Isosthenie bei Montaigne«) und Tobias Reinhardt (»Zenos Hand (Cicero, *Lucullus* §§ 144-6)«). Godarts Beitrag nimmt ebenfalls Blumenbergs Untersuchung der Anekdote vom Fall des Protophilosophen zum Ausgangspunkt, um zu zeigen, wie Montaigne sich die widersprüchlichen Anekdoten über Thales im Dienste der von ihm praktizierten »Technik einer literarischen Isosthenie« (S. 124) zunutze macht. Reinhardts philosophisch präzises *close reading* einer Textpassage bei Cicero hingegen ist einer von Zeno zum Zwecke der Illustration seiner Konzeption von Wissen verwendeten Geste gewidmet.

Den größten Ertrag für eine theoretisch-systematische Neuperspektivierung der Anekdote erbringt zweifellos der Aufsatz von Matthias Grandl (»Wie sich Anekdoten kommentieren. Theorie einer ›Affordanz‹ der Anekdote (nach H. Blumenberg, L. Sciascia und M.T. Cicero)«) mit seinem originellen Versuch, das auf den Wahrnehmungspsychologen James Jerome Gibson (Gibson 1979) zurückgehende Konzept der ›Affordanz‹ auf literarische Phänomene zu übertragen, um so zu zeigen, wie eine »der Anekdote ein-codierte Forderung nach einem spezifischen Umgang mit ihr« (S. 209) die Kommentatoren von Anekdoten dazu verführt, selbst in ein anekdotisches Schreiben zu verfallen. Diese ›automimetische Tendenz‹, der zufolge Anekdoten immer neue Anekdoten zeugen, demonstriert Grandl in virtuos-komparatistischer Manier, indem er sich mit Hans Blumenberg, Leonardo Sciascia und Cicero auf drei auf den ersten Blick eher disparate Autoren bezieht.

Den Einsatz- und Endpunkt der zweiten Sektion des Bandes, die einen weiten historischen Bogen zwischen dem 13. und dem 19. Jahrhundert aufspannt, markieren die Aufsätze von Falk Quenstedt (»Mediation neuen Wissens. Anekdoten in Marco Polos *Divisament dou monde* und dessen deutschsprachigen Fassungen«) und Inka Mülder-Bach (»Einzelfall, Exempel, Ausnahme: Spielräume des Anekdotischen bei Fontane«). Quenstedt zeigt in Anlehnung an Stephen Greenblatt (Greenblatt 1991), dass Marco Polos *Divisament dou monde* in seiner italo-französischen Fassung eine »Mediatorenfunktion hinsichtlich des für ein euro-mediterranes Publikum fundamental neuen und insofern fremden Wissens über die Mongolen« (S. 94) gehabt hat, aber auch wie diese Vermittler- und Integrationsfunktion im Zuge der Übersetzungen des Textes ins Deutsche verloren ging. Die Flexibilität der Wissensform der Anekdote erweist sich so als ambivalent: Was sie »zur Mediation und zum Transfer neuen Wissens befähigt, ist somit auch Einsatzpunkt von dessen Negation«, resümiert Quenstedt (S. 103). Zu einer Problematisierung des exemplarischen Status anekdotischen Wissens gelangt auch Mülder-Bach in ihrer Untersuchung der Anekdote als Erzähl- und Wissensform im Werk Fontanes, indem sie unter Bezug auf Figuren der Ausnahme und der Wiederholung bei Agamben und Kierkegaard einen Schwund an Eigentlichkeit und ein zunehmendes Auseinanderklaffen von Individuellem und Allgemeinem im Spätwerk Fontanes konstatiert.

Interessanterweise lässt sich eine nicht unähnliche Tendenz zur Problematisierung der exemplarischen Geltung anekdotischen Wissens nach der Darstellung von Frank Wittchow (»Vom *exemplum* zur Anekdote? Das Erbe der Annalistik bei Caesar, Livius und Tacitus«) auch schon in der antiken historiographischen Tradition beobachten, womit eine weitere interessante Querverbindung zwischen den Artikeln des Bandes bezeichnet wäre. In seiner Analyse einer sich im Übergang von der Republik zur Kaiserzeit vollziehenden »Transformation […] des historischen Wissens« (S. 56) arbeitet Wittchow als deren markantes Kennzeichen einen Bedeutungsverlust des *exemplum* zugunsten der zunehmenden Produktion von Anekdoten heraus, die sich durch ihre ironische Haltung gegenüber der Idee, dass Geschichte Handlungsanweisungen zu vermitteln imstande sei, auszeichnen. Ironisch zu verstehen ist ebenso die von dem Künstler Ad Reinhardt in seinem Lebenslauf praktizierte Relationierung individual-biographischer und historischer Ereignisse, was in dessen Rezeption nach Werner Buschs Darstellung in dem letzten Artikel des Bandes (»Ad Reinhardts Lebenslauf und seine schwarzen Bilder«) zu nicht wenigen Missverständnissen Anlass gegeben hat.

Das Verhältnis von Leben und Wissen zieht sich mit wechselnden Akzentuierungen wie ein roter Faden durch die Beiträge des Bandes. Ein wenig deutlicher hätte dieser Konnex in der von den Herausgeber*innen verfassten Einleitung profiliert sein können. Dass in deren Überschrift, »Epistemische Konstruktionen des (Auto)Biographischen in antiken und modernen Texten«, die ›Anekdote‹ überraschenderweise überhaupt nicht eigens Erwähnung findet, wird dagegen an keiner Stelle begründet, sondern offenbar als evident hingenommen. Die Gesichtspunkte, unter denen die Herausgeber*innen dann eine Ordnung in das unübersichtliche Feld anekdotischen Wissens von der Antike bis zur Gegenwart zu bringen versuchen, stehen in keinem unmittelbar erkennbaren Zusammenhang zum Aufbau des Bandes. Die konzeptuelle Untergliederung in die Bereiche »Materialität und Medialität von Anekdoten«, »Wissensoikonomien« und »Modi negativen Transfers« mag darum für die projektinterne Forschungsarbeit im Kontext des SFB relevant gewesen sein, zur Erhellung der Aufsätze des Sammelbandes trägt sie dagegen wenig bei. Zumal die Abschnitte der Einleitung nicht immer einlösen, was deren Überschriften verheißen, so etwa, wenn unter »Materialität und Medialität von Anekdoten« im Wesentlichen Fragen nach den Kriterien für die Zugehörigkeit zur Gattung und nach der Unterscheidung von angrenzenden Kleinformen, nach der Selbst- und Fremdreferentialität der Anekdote sowie nach der Autorschaft diskutiert werden. Wenn sich jedoch der leitende Gedanke von Matthias Grandls Entwurf einer Affordanz-Theorie der Anekdote darauf beläuft, dass sich über Anekdoten nur anekdotisch etwas Substantielles sagen lässt, dann wäre es nur konsequent, dass der Versuch, auf einer abstrakt-theoretischen Ebene über die Anekdote zu sprechen, von der Schwierigkeit zeugt, Allgemeines vom Einzelnen zu sagen und sauber zwischen Objekt- und Metasprache zu trennen. Ganz im Sinne ihrer Kommentator*innen bringt die

Anekdote somit Bewegung auch in die literatur- und kulturwissenschaftlichen Versuche, sie in einer schematischen Ordnung zu erfassen.

Literaturverzeichnis

Blumenberg, Hans (1983): »Glossen zu Anekdoten.« In: *Akzente. Zeitschrift für Literatur* 30, S. 28-41.

Blumenberg, Hans (1984): »Verfehlungen. Glossen zu Anekdoten.« In: *Akzente. Zeitschrift für Literatur* 31, S. 390-396.

Blumenberg, Hans (1988): »Nächtlicher Anstand. Glossen zu Anekdoten.« In: *Akzente. Zeitschrift für Literatur* 35, S. 42-55.

Blumenberg, Hans (1987): *Das Lachen der Thrakerin. Eine Urgeschichte der Theorie.* Frankfurt a.M.: Suhrkamp.

Fineman, Joel (1989): »The History of the Anecdote: Fiction and Fiction.« In: *The New Historicism.* Hrsg. von H. Aram Veeser. London, New York: Routledge, S. 49-76.

Fleming, Paul (2011): »The perfect story: Anecdote and exemplarity in Linnaeus and Blumenberg.« In: *Thesis Eleven* 104, S. 72-86.

Fleming, Paul (2012): »On the Edge of Non-Contingency: Anecdotes and the Lifeworld.« In: *Telos* 158, S. 21-35.

Gibson, James J. (1979): *The Ecological Approach to Visual Perception.* Boston: Houghton Mifflin.

Gilly, Florenz (2018): »Anekdote.« In: *Enzyklopädie der kleinen Formen* [Audio-Enzyklopädie des Podcasts *microform*], abrufbar unter: www.kleine-formen.de/enzyklopaedie-anekdote, Berlin.

Greenblatt, Stephen (1988): *Shakespearean Negotiations. The Circulation of Social Energy in Renaissance England.* Oxford : Clarendon.

Greenblatt, Stephen (1991): *Marvelous Possessions. The Wonder of the New World.* Chicago: The University of Chicago Press.

Möller, Melanie (Hg.) (2015): *Prometheus gibt nicht auf. Antike Welt und modernes Leben in Hans Blumenbergs Philosophie.* Paderborn: Fink.

Moser, Christian/Möller, Reinhard M. (Hg.) (2022): *Anekdotisches Erzählen: Zur Geschichte und Poetik einer kleinen Form.* Berlin: De Gruyter.

Schäfer, Rudolf (1982): *Die Anekdote. Theorie – Analyse – Didaktik.* München: Oldenbourg.

Schwindt, Jürgen Paul (Hg.) (2009): *Was ist eine philologische Frage? Beiträge zur Erkundung einer theoretischen Einstellung.* Frankfurt a.M.: Suhrkamp.

Zill, Rüdiger (2014a): »Anekdote.« In: *Blumenberg lesen. Ein Glossar.* Hrsg. von Robert Buch und Daniel Weidner. Berlin: Suhrkamp 2014, S. 26-42.

Zill, Rüdiger (2014b): »Minima historia. Die Anekdote als philosophische Form.« In: *Zeitschrift für Ideengeschichte* 8, S. 33-46.

KULTURWISSENSCHAFTLICHE ZEITSCHRIFT

Herausgegeben von der Kulturwissenschaftlichen Gesellschaft (KWG)

Die *Kulturwissenschaftliche Zeitschrift* versteht sich als ein offenes Forum der kulturwissenschaftlichen Debatte, in dem historische wie gegenwartskulturelle Themen, Theorien und Forschungsansätze aus allen Bereichen und Strömungen der Kulturwissenschaften vorgestellt und verhandelt werden. Neben Tagungsberichten und Rezensionen versammelt die KWZ halbjährlich mehrere durch ein doppeltblindes Peer-Review-Verfahren qualitätsgesicherte Aufsätze in deutscher oder englischer Sprache sowie einen Gastbeitrag zu aktuellen fachbezogenen Trends oder Forschungsgegenständen. Neben den regulären Ausgaben erscheinen pro Jahr 1–2 Schwerpunkthefte, die von Gastherausgeberschaften begleitet werden.

Zur interdisziplinär besetzten Redaktion gehören die Linguistin *Nina Kalwa* (Karlsruher Institut für Technologie), der Literatur- und Medienwissenschaftler *Lars Koch* (TU Dresden), die Amerikanistin und Kulturwissenschaftlerin *Nicole Maruo-Schröder* (Universität Koblenz), der Literaturwissenschaftler *Bernhard Stricker* (TU Dresden), die Amerikanistin *Maria Mothes* (Universität Koblenz) und der Germanist *Hendrik Groß* (TU Dresden).

WISSENSCHAFTLICHER BEIRAT:

Claudia Blümle
Professorin für Geschichte und Theorie der Form am Institut für Kunst- und Bildgeschichte der Humboldt-Universität zu Berlin

Astrid Fellner
Professorin für North American Literary and Cultural Studies an der Universität des Saarlandes

Stephan Moebius
Professor für soziologische Theorie und Ideengeschichte an der Karl-Franzens-Universität Graz

Thomas Stodulka
Juniorprofessor für Sozial- und Kulturanthropologie mit Schwerpunkt Psychologische Anthropologie an der FU Berlin

Tanja Thomas
Professorin für Medienwissenschaft mit dem Schwerpunkt Transformationen der Medienkultur an der Eberhard Karls Universität Tübingen

Niels Werber
Professor für Neuere Deutsche Literaturwissenschaft an der Universität Siegen

Vorschläge für Beitragsmanuskripte werden erbeten an:
manuskripte@kulturwissenschaftlichezeitschrift.de

Vorschläge für Rezensionsmanuskripte werden erbeten an:
rezensionen@kulturwissenschaftlichezeitschrift.de

Bei Fragen wenden Sie sich gerne an die Redaktion unter:
redaktion@kulturwissenschaftlichezeitschrift.de

Felix Meiner Verlag GmbH, Richardstraße 47, D-22081 Hamburg
Tel. +49 (40) 29 87 56-0 · vertrieb@meiner.de · www.meiner.de/kwz